# The Milliner's
# Apprentice

*A typical family portrait, showing the wedding of Alec Haigh in the 1920s. Arthur William and Sarah Eleanor are sitting to the left of the bridegroom and Hilda and Joe Taylor are standing behind them. Winnie is sitting at Arthur William's feet. Ella is sitting on the far left of the second row, the only lady to be wearing a white dress.*

# The Milliner's Apprentice

## GIRLHOOD IN EDWARDIAN YORKSHIRE

HAZEL WHEELER

SUTTON PUBLISHING

First published in the United Kingdom in 1997 by
Sutton Publishing Limited . Phoenix Mill
Thrupp . Stroud . Gloucestershire . GL5 2BU

British Library Cataloguing in Publication Data
A catalogue record for this book is available from the British Library

ISBN 0-7509-1330-4

*Cover illustrations: front; clockwise from top: Ella Haigh, Sarah Eleanor Haigh and
Hilda Haigh; Ernie Haigh, Hilda's brother who was killed in the First World War; an
example of typical Edwardian femininity, the winner of the Daily Mirror
International Beauty Contest, Miss Grace Lamont; Hilda on her first day as a
milliner's apprentice.*

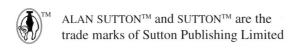 ALAN SUTTON™ and SUTTON™ are the
trade marks of Sutton Publishing Limited

Typeset in 11/12 pt Erhardt.
Typesetting and origination by
Sutton Publishing Limited.
Printed in Great Britain by
Ebenezer Baylis, Worcester.

# Contents

1. Tales My Mother Told Me     *1*

2. Characters     *6*

3. Starting School     *11*

4. A Country Playtime     *16*

5. The Arm of the Law     *20*

6. Another B-A-B-Y     *22*

7. Barnaby Fair     *26*

8. The Village Blacksmith     *30*

9. Home Remedies     *32*

10. Scarlet Fever Hospital     *35*

11. Whose Turn to Visit Aunt Louie?     *37*

12. Willie, the 'Boy' at Ripley Castle     *40*

13. Easter     *44*

14. In Shadow Pantomime Land     *47*

15. Christmas Joys     *51*

16. William, Footman at Brawith Hall     *56*

17. Shops and Shopping     *63*

18. The Surprise     *66*

*19. The Girls' Friendly Society*      *69*

*20. The Empire Day Prize*      *73*

*21. A New Beginning*      *79*

*22. The Milliner's Apprentice*      *83*

*23. War News*      *93*

*24. Stormy Weather*      *101*

*25. Hilda, a Wartime Post Girl*      *107*

*26. Rough Rider for Lord Furness*      *113*

*27. Clem Mustill Remembered*      *116*

# Acknowledgements

Many thanks to Bamforth's postcards, the late Clem Mustill, his son, Lord Justice Michael Mustill, and my cousin, Margaret Franks, for lending me the portrait of 'Uncle Willie', her father; also to the late Joe Boddy and *The Queen* for lending me the funeral number of 1910.

My special thanks also to *The Yorkshire Post* who published a photograph of Hilda in 1971, when she returned to Boroughbridge to stay at the Crown Hotel for Christmas; many of her old friends wrote, and were reunited as a result. Thanks to all those who provided hospitality and so much enjoyment, including the late Mrs Ethel Hope and Mrs Kathleen Slack. Grateful thanks to all, but most of all to the inspiring memory of my late mother, Hilda, the milliner's apprentice.

# CHAPTER 1

# Tales My Mother Told Me

Fairy tales are enchanting, but I always find that true stories are even better. In the 1930s when our village shop in Deighton, near Huddersfield, was closed for the day, and we drew our chairs up to the fire in wintertime, my mother loved to relive her Edwardian childhood. Her mother, my Grandma Haigh, had instilled into Hilda Margaret that, because she was born six hours after Queen Victoria died, she was most likely to be the reincarnation of the dead queen. Quite a rapid reincarnation one would think, but this did give her a sense of dignity and importance for the rest of her life: 23 January 1901 was a very important day!

*Hilda, showing her penchant for fashionable headgear.*

But there was another side to those elegantly dressed Edwardians; their love of gaiety and the music-hall, and Hilda had those qualities in full measure. When she wasn't recounting her life peacefully spent in Jasmine Cottage, New Row, Boroughbridge, North Yorkshire, as one of the village constable's children, she loved to play the piano in the front room over our grocer's shop. Hilda possessed a superb contralto voice and used it to marvellous effect, playing and singing those sentimental, dramatic, and often silly music-hall melodies. The piano stool was completely crammed with sheet music.

She never forgot the happiness of being a milliner's apprentice after leaving the village school, so it wasn't surprising that one of her favourite songs was,

> Put on Your Tat-Ta, little girlie,
> Do, do what I want you to!
> Far from the busy hurly-burly,
> I've got lots to say to you.
> My head's completely twirly-whirly,
> My girl I want you to be–
> So put on your tat-ta, your pretty little tat-ta,
> And come out a tat-ta with me.

All these songs were sung with great verve and vivacity and it was no wonder that customers adored coming into the shop on any small excuse, just to hear those Edwardian songs from the upstairs room.

The next piece might be 'When You Come Home', which had beautiful words and a beautiful tune.

> Birds in the garden, all day long, singing for me their happy song
> Flowers in the sunshine, wind and dew, all of them speak to me of you;
> You that I long for, near or far, you that I follow like a star,
> Day may be weary, weary and long, you will come home at evensong
> When you come home, dear, all with be fair,
> Home is not home if you are not there;
> You in my heart, dear, you at my side,
> When you come home at eventide.

Hilda's voice, becoming lower and more dramatic for the final verse, would often cause whoever was listening to shed a few tears, but it didn't do for Hilda to remain too serious for long. Quick as a flash the mood, and song, would change. Up from the piano stool, adopting the pose of Burlington Bertie, strutting across the floor, 'with my gloves on my hand, then I stroll down again with them 'orf – I'm all airs and graces, correct easy paces, Without food so long I forget where my face is – I'm Bert, Bert, I haven't a shirt, but my people are County you know—Nearly everyone knows me – from Smith to Lord Roseberry, I'm Burlington Bertie from Bow, ho-ho.'

Those songs were ideal for flirting. The handsome young vicar who came to the shop occasionally for Sunday dinner after morning service was a fan of Hilda.

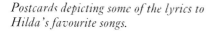

**Honeysuckle and the Bee.**

You are my Honeysuckle, I am the Bee,
I'd like to sip the honey sweet
From those red lips you see,
I love you dearly, dearly, and I
Want you to love me,
You are my Honeysuckle,
I am the Bee.

Words by permission of FRANCIS, DAY, & HUNTER.

*Postcards depicting some of the lyrics to*
*Hilda's favourite songs.*

What a delightful diversion after the Yorkshire pudding to be invited upstairs and regaled with the piano tinkling, flashing hazel eyes and that voice. He certainly didn't object to:

> You are my honeysuckle, I am the bee,
> I'd like to sip the honey sweet
> From those red lips you see.
> I love you dearly, dearly, and I
> Want you to love me–
> You are my honey, honeysuckle
> I am the bee.

Oh, how I longed to have lived in those dear, dead Edwardian days but hearing about them was the next best thing. Dad frequently joined in after the washing-up was done and a cosy, magical world of music was created until it was time for afternoon service.

'Love's Old Sweet Song' was not thought unseemly for a Sunday repertoire and out it came from the piano stool, Hilda's long 'piano fingers' bringing out the nostalgic feeling.

> Just a song at twilight, when the lights are low,
> And the flickering shadows, softly come and go,
> Tho' the heart be weary, sad the day and long,
> Still to us at twilight, comes Love's old song,
> Comes Love's old, sweet, song.

*The High Street, Boroughbridge, with the Greyhound Hotel on the left.*

If the local bobby popped in for a chat while on his beat, Hilda jauntily, flirtingly, would tickle him under the chin, launching into the song that reminded her of her dad, village constable of Boroughbridge and her hero.

> Oh, dearie me, how my poor heart does beat
> Longing for the day when that Bobby comes again,
> With his red rosy cheeks, and his heart that is ever true–
> He is the darling of my heart – that Bonny Boy in Blue.

Where else could 'Bobby' Ward get a glass of Tizer, a few Huntley and Palmer biscuits, a rest on the shop Bentwood chair with the little holes in the seat making a pattern, and an Edwardian music-hall turn into the bargain? 'Come on then, Hilda, let's have another,' he always coaxed.

Her dad, the one-time Police Constable Haigh, was also fond of poetry, but Hilda could only partly remember one poem, 'He was a Careful Man'.

> He was a careful man, where'ere he went, 'twas his intent,
> To be a careful man. In June he wore an overcoat, to guard against the storm
> And left it off in wintertime in case it should turn warm
> He never went in Hansom cabs for fear the horses kicked . . .

*PC Haigh, Hilda's father, when he was working in Huddersfield at L.B. Holliday's as a security officer.*

Hilda quite enjoyed washing the steps and finishing them off with a broad edging of yellow scouring stone. That was a task for Fridays. Everything had to be shipshape for weekends, as though the community expected some celebrity such as the King to emerge on the bridge some Saturday.

But there were only the same characters around at the weekends. One old man had a perpetual limp. The tale went round that he'd been dropped when he was a baby and ever since, his hip or something had never been quite right.

Of course, there used to be such harsh winters that it's a miracle anyone remained upright. Some recollected, in the winter of 1895, skating down the river from Roecliffe to Boroughbridge to buy the groceries.

Frankie Foster told a tale about another familiar character who managed to wriggle out of a pair of handcuffs. His withered hand came on soon after that little manoeuvre.

PC Haigh was one of the most familiar figures around in those early years of the century. Tall and lean, with a waxed moustache, he could tap backsides when necessary yet in his more usual, and amiable moods, often paused to stroke a cat sunning itself on a wall. For some unknown reason a cat, to him, was a 'titty puss'. Many a lad sniggered behind his back on hearing Haigh crooning, 'Now then, titty puss, what then, titty me love?'

Similarly with pigs. Leaning over a farmyard wall he whistled softly to the fleshy, snorting animals, grunting their way through mud baths and mountains of feed. 'Hullo there, Pig Jack.'

Patience was his strongest virtue. One evening, coming up to 5 November, he came across a lad throwing fireworks at a shop door on the corner of Fishergate and High Street. Being young and nippy Freddie Bendelow managed to escape PC Haigh by vaulting over a wall near the cemetery. Then he made his mistake. He climbed a tree. Haigh arrived at the foot of it and called up, 'All right, me lad, I can wait until you come down.' And he did.

Only when the church clock struck midnight did Freddie realize the 'Bobby' would wait forever if need be. Frozen stiff he descended to face the policeman's wrath. A twist of the ear and the admonition, 'Now don't ever throw any more fireworks, it's a stupid thing to do and could have caused a fire', was all that he received.

But worse was to come when the culprit arrived home in Roecliffe. His father was waiting behind the door with a belt, which was used when Freddie recounted what had happened. But young Bendelow admired the constable. 'He did what was right, and children have to be disciplined,' he said in later years.

PC Haigh himself wasn't above reproach. On one rare occasion, at Christmas that same year, he and Dick Carass, the village joker, teamed up to commit a seasonable 'crime'. Arthur Petty, the plumber, observed by the two conspirators, had gone out on Christmas night with his family. Stealthily, they clambered in through the plumber's pantry window, making off with the remains of the Christmas goose. Hurrying off to the Malt Shovel, one of the many public houses, they finished off the bird.

Next morning a red-faced, flustered Mr Petty burst into the police station to report the theft. At the sight of 'Bobby' Haigh's beaming face, light dawned on him. 'Oh, so it was you, you old devil was it?' he laughed.

A good, well-meaning young woman called Miss Green was left a sum of money by her father. She used it to open the Boroughbridge Boys' Club. A billiard table was installed and Joe Petch, a cripple of small stature, took it upon himself to keep order in the club.

The lads christened Joe 'The Foreman', and although he was short-tongued as well as being a dwarf, when he called for 'Thilence' there was silence. He warned the boys, 'You must not tell untruths, or God won't love you.' At half-past nine he called, 'Gentlemen, the lights are about to be extinguished.' It was considered late enough for teenagers to be out of the club at this time. Policeman Haigh usually popped in to make sure the lads were behaving themselves.

*Revd Bingham and Joe Petch (standing, second row, far left) with members of the church choir.*

---

# JOHN BACON,

## *Grocer, Provision and Seed Merchant,*

## BOROUGHBRIDGE.

---

### THE OLDEST ESTABLISHED IN THE DISTRICT.

---

*An advertisement for John Bacon's grocery business. This is the name that caused Hilda so much embarrassment when she was out shopping.*

Once the group went to Scarborough for an outing. 'It's a very expensive place, Scarborough,' complained Joe. 'I hadn't been there five minutes before bang went a halfpenny.' He had indulged in an ice-cream cornet. The club was also used as a bank. Miss Green used to save the few pence the boys could put aside until there was enough to buy their mothers a present. The system worked. Whoever heard of vandalism and petty thieving when the words of Miss Green, Joe Petch, and PC Haigh were heeded?

Hilda, though married to grocer Joe Taylor in later years, could never get over her amazement that the grocer patronized by her family when she was a child was called Mr Bacon. How embarrassed she used to feel having to address him by that name, especially if that item was on the shopping list. One of his hands sloped to one side; a result, he maintained, of many years slicing his namesake by hand.

Animals figured among the village characters too; especially horses, and particularly old Ben, a whopping big Clydesdale. One day a steamroller broke down, and nothing managed to get it going again. 'Out o't way,' boomed Ben's proud master, 'and let our Ben get on wi't job.' One heave of the horse's powerful muscles and off the roller went.

Every New Year's Day Lady Lawson-Tancred distributed fruit to the poor, and local shopkeepers threw out red-hot halfpennies for children to scramble for in the fountain and horse troughs.

On the morning of 1 January Boroughbridge men decked themselves up with bits of straw, and walked round chanting:

> Lucky bird, Lucky bird, chuck, chuck, chuck,
> Master and Missus, it's time to get up.
> If you don't get up, you'll have no luck,
> Lucky bird, Lucky bird, chuck, chuck, chuck.

Although there were adequate drinking facilities in the village, with all the public houses, on one day of the year, at Barnaby Fair time, even ordinary houses could sell beer if they displayed a green branch in a prominent position. It could be either pushed through a window or hung from a nail on the door.

*Ella Haigh, Hilda's sister.*

A fellow who regularly drove a wagonette to Ripon market was invariably dead drunk on the way home. It didn't concern his passengers the least little bit, as the horses dutifully halted at all the usual stopping places. The man who hawked fish pushed a barrow to Knaresborough to make his purchases, then his cry rang out: 'Fine red herrings, guaranteed red-arsed 'uns.'

Doctor Daggett was the first man in the area to own a car and his patients viewed him with more awe than ever before after the acquisition of such a marvellous contraption. His daughter appeared to believe that what with her father being a doctor and having one of the new motor cars, she was entitled to treat her 'inferiors' in an autocratic manner.

'Good morning, Haigh,' she called out to Hilda's dad one morning as Hilda and Ella were walking with him down Horsefair. Arthur William was about to go into the usual deferentials of bowing and scraping before the young Madam, but Ella was quicker. 'Good morning, Daggett,' she spat back.

The constable may only have been earning perhaps a pound a week, but he surely earned everyone's respect. After all, the people's safety was in his hands. This was demonstrated when Sergeant Foster was writing out a charge against a man in custody. The man brought out a poker from beneath his jacket – Police Constable Haigh knocked him down and saved Foster's life. No wonder his family were proud of him.

# CHAPTER 3

# Starting School

Being next to the youngest child in the family, Hilda looked forward to joining the others at school. Many a time she sneaked out of the garden gate while her Mama was busy putting bread to rise in front of the fire or possing the washing.

Wash day, on a Monday, was busy from start to finish. On the evening before all the clothes were sorted, white ones, coloured ones, into separate piles. Some had to be scrubbed across a ridged board with a big bar of Hudson's soap. A peggy stick with long handle was used to press clothes up and down in the peggy tub, which was shaped like a barrel. At some part of the day a dolly blue was squeezed into the water to add extra whiteness, although I never knew why adding blue should make clothes whiter. Woollies were washed separately and then the mangling was done. The clothes were then hung on the line to blow in the breeze.

If the clothes were a bit too dry when they were brought in they were damped before ironing, then folded. Flat irons were put on the Yorkshire range fire to warm and held with a bit of old flannel. Finally, the clothes were aired on a huge fireguard and clothes-horse, and some over a creel hung from the ceiling. With all this going on it was easy for Hilda to scuttle across the lane and into the school yard without being noticed. In 1905, when Hilda was four years old at last, she was old enough to join the others at school. On her first day her mother tied a veil round her face to shield it from the raw January wind. She peered through the holes of the ancient lace curtain to see where she was going, and her sister Hannah christened her 'Lady Muriel'.

Children who lived at Minskip left school half an hour earlier than the rest of them in dark weather, to try and reach their homes while there was some daylight left. The teacher warned them to 'stick together' along the lonely lanes. Miss Randall rode to school on her bicycle, clad in an ankle-length maroon coloured overall with a big cape collar, black woollen stockings, lace-up boots and a grim expression.

Teachers were held in awe, with the pupils rushing to do their bidding. If they didn't, there was punishment, often by caning. One boy was held over a tutorial knee after an escapade one afternoon. Each time the cane contacted his coarse trousers such a cloud of dust rose up that both he and the teacher seemed liable to be obscured from view.

Hilda liked Mr Mawer but one day he ordered her to stand on one of the wooden forms for talking, instead of paying attention. How terrible she felt! She began to weep, hating to feel in disgrace, and her handkerchief became wet with tears. It wasn't long before the kindly schoolmaster gently told her she could get

*A Boroughbridge school group. Hilda is standing at the far left on the third row; she has two white ribbons in her hair. Ella is on the far right, wearing a big hat, with the teacher's arm around her.*

down again, and gave her his own big white handkerchief to mop up the remaining tears. They were friends once more and she vowed never to upset him again.

When Hilda moved up into Standard 2 she was taught by Miss Randall. One week the child had two large boils on her back and once again talking too much was her downfall. Miss Randall strode up behind her and gave Hilda a whacking thump on the back. Right on the boils, though she wasn't to know. They burst, and without so much as a by-your-leave Hilda raced out of the classroom and along the lane to home, sobbing with pain and humiliation.

Her mother immediately stopped what she was doing, put on her hat, coat and gloves, and stormed through the lane and into Miss Randall's classroom. Grabbing her by the shoulders, she hauled her into the presence of Mr Mawer, where Miss Randall had to apologize. After that, teacher and pupil got on very well indeed. Peace-offerings of apples, pears, and vegetables from the Haigh's orchard were accepted with gratitude and humility.

Tall stoves fuelled with coke kept the school heated in winter, the 'big boys' keeping them stoked up. A large fireguard surrounded them. Some children who lived quite a distance from school brought sandwiches for lunch, eating them at Mrs Haigh's who also brewed hot drinks for them. Eventually a room was equipped with a cooking stove and then the children could warm up soup on wintry days.

When Hilda's birthday drew near she asked her mother if she could invite Mr Mawer's daughter, Constance Mary, with her other friends to the cottage for tea.

Conscious of the Great Honour when the invitation was accepted, Hilda kept a tight grip on the hand of her prized guest and looked after Constance Mary as if she was a little God.

The children teased little Emily Robinson and said she would be locked up in the cells overnight if she didn't behave herself, but they would never have dreamed of threatening Mr Mawer's daughter with such a fate. Mrs Mawer came for her little daughter in the early evening and thanked Hilda very much for having her and taking such good care of her.

Only one other time at school did Hilda recall being told to go and stand in a corner, for talking too much again. The teacher's fur coat was hanging from a hook where the child stood, face turned away from the rest of the class. She started stroking the fur, and getting a little bit of comfort putting her head near the lovely warmth of it. By this time Hilda needed to go to the lavatory but, because she was in disgrace, she wasn't allowed to. Hilda couldn't wait any longer and was soon in trouble again.

'Fancy doing that so near my lovely fur coat!' the teacher admonished her. Once again Mrs Haigh heard about the incident. On went her coat, hat and gloves. She asked the teacher how she could be so cruel. Apologies were accepted, and assurances were made that it would never happen again.

There were no buses then, so if there was an invitation to tea after school the guests had to walk there and back. School friends Kathleen Morton and her brother and sister were among those who called at Jasmine Cottage for a warm drink during school dinnertime. The big black kettle was never off the Yorkshire range, ready to refresh whoever may call.

Some children earned a few coppers by doing jobs for people in the village. Lady Lawson-Tancred had a Rover car and Hilda's brother Alec used to wash it for her. Later on she taught him how to drive, he never had to pass an official test. Alec also cleaned the Lawson-Tancred family boots and pumped water for their baths as well as emptying 'muck bins' for Doctor Daggett. There was no time to be bored or to get into mischief.

When a lad had done an honest job, he expected to be rewarded for it. Unlike the esteemed 'upper-class type of person' who played fair with him, Alec once shovelled a load of coal in for a local man. When finished, there was not even a halfpenny recompense. Despite it being such a back-breaking job, Alec shovelled it all outside again. But his dad, PC Haigh, on hearing about this, immediately ordered his son to shovel it back in. He believed that youngsters ought to help others, whether a reward was forthcoming or not.

Despite having his 'backside cracked' more than once for misdemeanours, young Victor Styan regarded the constable as 'a good copper'. His father was a great friend of Arthur William and was the horsebreaker at Minskip, but friend or foe made no difference to PC Haigh, if punishment was deserved, it was meted out.

School friend Cissie Smallwood and her brother Sydney used to keep company with old Mr Mountain when school was over. Another of Hilda's brothers, Willie, went to Mr Mountain's home every evening to take the old gentleman's boots off so that he could retire to bed.

*Hilda (on the left), Ella (in the centre) and their cousin, Audrey Livesey, in the garden at Jasmine Cottage.*

Those Edwardian summers were so glorious, one could hardly blame the occasional truancy. A few boys were catching eels in the beck at St Helena when they should have been behind their desks at school. Some went swimming. There were no swimming lessons at school in those days, they simply swam by instinct in the river. Few missed the conjuror when he visited the school if they could help it or the great treat of a magic lantern show, which came to the Public Hall. Children had to pay only a copper or two, and their excitement was palpable as they eagerly awaited the first slide to be put on. There was also the thrill when the ragman was waiting for them to come hurtling out of school. 'Tell your mothers to bring out their old rags and I'll have a bit o' summat for thee when tha' comes back,' he bargained. The 'bit o' summat' was usually a bright, shiny, whirling windmill. How Hilda and her playmates longed for the wind to go boistering along, so they could run and skip in the playground with their windmill sails turning merrily. Hilda had transacted a business exchange and felt inordinately proud of herself when she raced home at teatime to show off her new treasure. Her mother was always there, with freshly baked bread and home-made jam, scones spread thickly with butter and a slice of Robin cake or Madeira loaf to finish off with.

Shuttlecock and battledore were favourite pastimes in springtime. One elderly show-off who enjoyed leaning over the schoolyard wall watching the games, once boasted that he could, 'eat owt wi' feathers on'. One of Hilda's chums presented him with her shuttlecock, then wished she hadn't. He ate it all, except for the wooden base.

Hopscotch was another popular pastime. Then, one never to be forgotten Easter, Hilda was presented with a huge wooden 'booler' and wooden stick. Her dad had engraved her name, Hilda Margaret Haigh, round the rim of the hoop in thick black pencil. She was then able to bool happily along with her brothers who had iron boolers.

October was the month children began 'chumping' for wood for the November bonfires. Halloween turned into November, with swirling mists and sharp, tangy mornings, a fitful sun occasionally peeping out briefly. Massive mutton stews were cooking slowly over the fire and the children gazed, starry-eyed, into the bow-windows of little shops that sold 'squibs', as Mischief Night and Bonfire Night arrived. Saturday pennies were spent on Catherine wheels, sparklers and rockets.

Hilda's mother would be busy turning out trays of golden parkin and making treacle toffee. Bought toffee can be scrumptious, but one is denied the delight of scraping warm leftovers straight from the oven into eager mouths. Next morning Hilda took a piece of parkin and some toffee, neatly wrapped, for the teacher. And Sarah Eleanor was rewarded by the annual acclamation from her husband, 'Ay lass, tha' art the best treacle toffee-maker in all England!' He adored to eat treacle toffee as he ambled round on his beat.

*St James's Square, Boroughbridge.*

# CHAPTER 4

# A Country Playtime

When school was over, playtime was sheer delight. The children enjoyed it all the more for not having any expensive toys. When most families had a large number of children there simply wasn't the money for them. But how their imaginations and the treasures of the countryside compensated! Children could be King Edward, with an old sheet as a Coronation cloak and a crown of old beads or wild flowers. A child could be King, Queen, Princess or fairy – anyone or anything at all. These immeasurable pleasures cost not a penny.

Hilda loved playing in the old stable in their orchard, keeping it clean as a new pin. It was her own little den, her palace. The residents of this 'kingdom' were the spades, rakes, hoes and forks. All were given names, written on bits of paper which were stuck on the implements so the inanimate 'children' wouldn't get mixed up. The spade was named Alfred, the elegant rake, Victoria. A squat little trowel was Toby. A hoe was called Edward.

*Examples of children's toys of the time. Hilda owned a doll very similar to the one in the left-hand picture.*

If they didn't know their multiplication tables when playing school, these garden schoolchildren were chastized verbally. But if they had learned them correctly they were taken outside for a walk. The few home-made rag dolls didn't ride in proper, shop-brought perambulators, but sat erect and proud in little 'bogeys' made by dads. These were simply constructed from discarded wooden orange boxes, which had been swooped upon with delight when the grocer was giving them away, with old pram wheels and shafts nailed on. They made admirable dolls' prams. Home-made sledges and 'trolley carts' provided hours of fun too.

Joy knew no bounds if a neighbour was throwing out an old table or ricketty chairs. They were installed in the stable and the children played at shops. Butter was a picture of a pat, imprinted with the face of a placid yellow cow, but from a paper or magazine. Dresses for sale in the 'drapery department' were also cut out from papers. Sometimes dolls' knitted outfits were exchanged or a few items from jumble sales ended up on the 'shop' table.

Perhaps Hilda's imagination was inherited from her mother, who, like Mr Micawber, always believed that something better would turn up for her beloved brood. If Hilda occasionally became disgruntled because some of the well-off girls went to Knaresborough Grammar School, travelling there by train, her mother thrust out her ample chest, the light of battle shining in her eyes. 'Perhaps in a little while, when there's more money, I'll get you a governess.'

*Ella, Sarah Eleanor and Hilda.*

That really would have been stretching the imagination too far, what with a family consisting of Hannah, Willie, George, Ernest, Alec, Hilda, Ella – infants Cissie and Stanley in the churchyard – and, later, Hannah's daughter Winnie to bring up.

But illusions of coming grandeur were sown in Hilda's mind and she practised being a governess on those wayward Alfreds and Adelaides in the stable. Grandma Haigh must have often wished her daughter was not given to such hoity-toity ways when a clean, starched, white pinafore was demanded every morning. And she wouldn't stir outside the cottage, except if playing in the garden, without her gloves.

Playtime in winter was equally delightful. In the cottage was a kind of wooden secretaire, a sloping piece of wood in great demand. Hilda enjoyed writing stories, often not bothering to get a piece of paper first. The children played noughts and crosses, drew stiff cats and dogs and carved their initials on the wood itself.

A highlight of the year was Sunday School Prize Giving Day. On that special day a fire was lit in the tiny front room, importantly named 'the boudoir' by Sarah Eleanor. This was in part to remind her policeman husband that she had French aristocracy in her blood and also if she felt his passions may be waning and required a bit of fanning into flame.

A huge brass nursery fireguard kept the great roaring fire safe in the blackleaded fireplace and a cosy blanket was thrown over the black horsehair sofa for when the children raced home with their book prizes.

In 1909 Hilda faced the worst moment of her life. She had longed for the moment when her requested book, *Granny's Wonderful Chair* would be hers and she could curl up, secure from the bleak midwinter outside, and be carried away in spirit to fairy places, while her mother toasted muffins for tea on the long toasting fork in front of the fire. Then the Sunday School Superintendent took her on one side. 'My dear, would you mind changing *Granny's Wonderful Chair* with Ada – she has had her book before.'

What could she do? She didn't want to be mean, yet she had so longed for that particular book. Tears clouded her eyes. 'Oh, but I did want this one Sir,' Hilda stammered. The gentle, whiskery-faced man patted her head. 'Never mind, you keep your book. We'll find someone else to change with Ada.' Her gratitude knew no bounds, she thanked him profusely, and even dropped a little curtsey.

Heart thumping with relief and anticipated pleasure, she ran home, clutching the beloved book. Tremulously, she turned the pages and wrote inside, 'Hilda Haigh, Boro'bridge Sunday School, Xmas 1909'. The fire in the grate burned brightly, the curtains were drawn shutting out the December bleakness and Hilda began to read. What wonderful stories were told! Unlike modern children's books which often have more illustrations than text, *Granny's Wonderful Chair* had only three black and white pictures. Hilda treasured it all her life, reading it to my brother Philip and me years later.

My favourite story is the one about brothers Scrub and Spare, poorest of all in the midst of a bleak moor in the north country. The door was always open, for there was no window, and the hut was made of clay and wattles. By giving their last crust of bread to a cuckoo, good fortune came to them. Of course, there's much more to the story than that, but stories for children in those days had a moral to them and must have helped guide the young, by example, to live decent lives.

The book was published by S.W. Partridge & Co., and listed inside were other titles, such as the 'True Grit' series including *A Captive in the Zulu Camp*, *Stirring Sea Fights*, *A Book for British Boys* and *Smoking Flax* by Silas K. Hocking. Handsomely bound in cloth boards, those titles marked with an asterisk were also bound with gilt edges, these cost 3*s* each.

New 5*s* library books included *True unto Death: A Story of Russian Life* by E.F. Pollard. In the 5*s* 'Empire' series was included, *Not Out! A Public School Story* and *Playing the Game: Another Public School Story* both by Kent Carr. For 3*s* 6*d*, *Partridge's Children's Annual*, compiled by the editor of *The Children's Friend*, could be bought, or *The Story of the Bible, arranged in Simple Style for Young People*. The *Pilgrim's Progress* was another popular Sunday School prize book.

Partridge's Eighteenpenny series of 'Charming Stories for Holiday and Fireside Reading' included such titles as *A Great Patience*, *A Late Repentance* and *A Noble Champion*. Partridge's 'Popular Illustrated Monthlies' included *The British Workman*, a fully illustrated magazine containing articles and stories on temperance, thrift and much information of value to the sons of toil. There was also the *Band of Hope Review*, which was the 'Leading Temperance Periodical for the Young', containing serials and short stories, concert recitations and prize competitions.

Another treasured Sunday School prize was *Alice in Wonderland*, with an authentic Edwardian Alice wearing black woollen stockings, a low-waisted dress and with huge bows keeping her ringlets in place. In fading ink at the front of this particular book was written: 'Prize for Texts and Attendance at Boroughbridge Sunday School. December, 1908. Hilda Margaret Haigh.' Other well-loved prizes were *The Life of Jesus* and *Little Bo-Peep*.

Jasmine Cottage must have had plenty of Bibles. By the will of Philip, Lord Wharton, who died 4 February 1696, he left to his Trustees certain estates in Yorkshire, the proceeds of which were to be devoted each year to the distribution of Bibles and other books. By the terms of the will the 1st, 15th, 25th, 37th, 101st, 113th and 145th Psalms should be learnt, if possible, by the recipient. Hilda was presented with her Lord Wharton Bible in 1910 and Ella received hers in 1916.

Somewhere along life's winding highway *The Life of Jesus* and *Little Bo-Peep* were lost. But in my bookcase still are *Granny's Wonderful Chair*, *Alice in Wonderland*, *Our Empire Story* (presented on the occasion of my mother winning the Empire Day Essay in 1915) and the two Bibles. The stories in them are still as fresh as the wild violets Hilda used to gather in those carefree Edwardian playtimes.

# CHAPTER 5

# The Arm of the Law

Jasmine Cottage was situated right next to the police station. Hilda's dad, Arthur William Haigh, was a great believer in fresh air and exercise and used to line his family up before an open window, winter or summer alike. Seven chests were exhorted to 'breathe in – hold it – again', while he counted up to ten. Then the children had to breathe out, slowly.

There should have been nine chests, but the first born, Stanley, and the eldest sister, Cissie, died in infancy before they had the opportunity to receive any of their policeman father's rigorous training. Hilda often used to think about those tiny babies lying in their graves. How awful to die in infancy, and yet, there is also so much to be endured when life itself often holds such sorrow and hardship.

No carpets were allowed in the cottage, they weren't considered healthy, so huge pegged rugs took the chill off the linoleum. As the children grew older their dad delighted in teaching them 'the tricks of the trade', how to heave dumb-bells and deal with the 'criminal fraternity'.

Drunks were regularly housed in the police cell, sleeping it off on a wooden bed, with a wooden 'pillow' and rough dark blankets to cover themselves with. When the Sergeant was away on holiday, leaving Arthur William in charge, Hilda loved to go inside the station and swizzle round and round on his big swivel chair. She felt a great sense of power surging beneath her white starched pinafore to be in such a seat of authority. A Mrs Fawcett was forever getting drunk down at the Black Bull and PC Haigh used to coax her gently back to the police station to brew her a cup of tea to help 'pull herself together'. But even the arm of the law can sometimes find themselves in peculiar circumstances. One morning PC Haigh was downstairs in the cells seeing to the prisoners. With him went the Sergeant's son, young Frankie Foster. Arthur William was due out on his beat shortly after, but when that time came, he was nowhere to be seen. Morning wore on into afternoon, but the constable was still missing.

Sergeant Foster called to his son. 'Frankie, nip through the hedge and ask Mrs Haigh if the constable isn't well.' Then Frankie remembered – he had clanged the new, self-locking cell doors shut, trapping Hilda's dad an innocent prisoner in one cell. He looked quite sheepish when his superior freed him, with profuse apologies.

Frankie was a firm favourite with Hilda. As a toddler she used to peer through the privet hedge lisping, 'Frankie, Frankie, come and talk to t' hedge.' She loved it if he invited her to play inside his house. She used to stare for ages at the two big white china dogs which gazed resolutely ahead on the high mantelpiece. Another of Mrs Foster's delights was a row of blue and white willow-patterned plates, kept on a rack in the kitchen. There was nothing as grand in the Haigh cottage, but they did have a prickly black horsehair sofa on which the children's dad stretched out full length when not on duty, the prickles softened by an old plush tablecloth.

To shut out the busy domestic scene when he wanted a snooze he draped his brass-buttoned police coat over a chair back, placed his big boots at the ready on the red-ochred floor, and spread the newspaper over his face. When rhythmic snores wafted the *Daily News* gently up and down, Hilda and her sister Ella, always prone to giggles, began to take advantage of his slumbers. Chasing each other round the square, scrubbed wooden table or seeing who could touch one of their dad's twitching toes without waking him up.

PC Haigh, however, was not such a deep sleeper for all his snores. Also, even with his own brood, his word was law. All he needed to do to send them scurrying quietly to their books, or outside to play, was to fling out a bony hand. 'Silence!' he thundered and silence there would be. There came a time, however, when both he and Sergeant Foster were themselves stilled to a quivering silence by a Power even more formidable than themselves. An old crone, who lived alone in a tumbledown cottage, complained at the police station that there was a ghost in her room which made unaccountable bangings. Could one of them attend to the matter?

Neither of those two worthies had ever had such a request before and queried the suitability of themselves for such a task. Surely the Vicar —? 'I'm not asking him and having him thinking I'm a looney,' snapped the woman, pulling her tatty shawl tighter round her scrawny shoulders. 'This is a matter for the police.'

Wisely, the arm of the law decided to tackle the job in daylight – and together. One or two who were in the know as to the purpose of the visit, hung about in the lane, anxious to hear news of the apparition. No one did find out who or what accounted for the unexplained noises in that lonely cottage. But two figures in navy blue came out quicker than they went in and the story goes that both PC Haigh and Sergeant Foster were running for dear life, and white as new dishcloths.

When questioned about the incident, Arthur William was either too busy to discuss it, or in urgent need of 'a bit of hush'. In later years, when she was old enough to understand the peccadillos of the world, Hilda found out that the ghost story was only a fiction made up by the lonely woman.

The Gossips said that it was only an excuse so she could get a man in the house.

# CHAPTER 6

# Another B-A-B-Y

Even at the age of fourteen, mother told me she was absolutely convinced that babies grew on gooseberry bushes. Families were kept in complete ignorance about the subjects that didn't, or shouldn't, concern them. Older brothers and sisters could do little to enlighten them about the Mysteries of Life, as they often went into service at big houses or stately homes after leaving school; sometimes as early as thirteen.

Willie went on to be a footman at Ripley Castle, Hannah to be a cook, first at Kirby Hill then to Bamborough Castle. George, prior to joining the police force, became a butcher's boy, handsome in a blue and white striped apron, riding his bike through the cobbled streets, wicker basket full of prime red meat covered with a spotless tea towel. How proud their mother was of her still completely innocent brood.

*George Haigh, Hilda's brother. He eventually followed in his father's footsteps and joined the police force. He later lived in Harrogate.*

*Sarah Eleanor, Hilda's mother, in her later years.*

Although prams were refilled with regularity, it seemed quite natural, as gooseberry bushes were plentiful in most gardens. No one saw much of newly-born infants as the vogue for putting them out in all weathers had not yet begun. Even in the perfect summers of 1910 and thereabout, Hilda remembered seeing infants muffled up in woollen shawls and hand-knitted bonnets. Air, clean, pure country air, unpolluted by traffic fumes, was regarded by mothers as a dangerous commodity, to be kept away from their little ones at all cost.

Even with these precautions, many did not live long enough to emerge from the pram stage. The funeral bell announced the final journey of a baby or child by tolling three times; a woman merited seven, a man, nine. Hilda and her friends were saddened when they heard the bell tolling three and whispered to each other, 'Oh, a baby's died.' Tears were not far away as they watched a horse and cart bearing a little coffin to the church.

The majority of couples hadn't much idea how to avoid repeated pregnancies. It was simply taken as a matter of course when another baby arrived. It was rare for a baby not to be breast-fed for as long as possible. Economy was the watchword, there being no prop such as Family Allowance or free school dinners.

It wasn't considered wrong for parents to have an infant in the same bed as themselves, maybe some thought it an excellent means of birth control. Many thought it quite unthinkable to leave a baby on its own, and the arrangement saved many a dispute as to who should step out onto the cold linoleum-covered bedroom floor to tend to the crying child.

A large wooden cradle was regularly occupied in Jasmine Cottage. Once, when Sarah Eleanor had a sore finger, she had to rock the cradle with her foot and prepare vegetables for dinner with her sound fingers. There was no mattress in the cradle, just layers of blankets cut from the best parts of old ones, with a blanket stitch hem. There were no special high-chairs for the Haigh babies. When they reached the 'sitting at the table' stage they were tied firmly to an ordinary chair with a scarf.

A police constable's wage didn't run to expensive toys, yet what pleasure and sense of achievement was derived from making dolls and other toys for themselves. Mrs Haigh created unique, life-like monster dolls out of old clothes which were stuffed with old woollen stockings and had boot buttons for eyes. One which had become grubby through many caresses was washed and mangled then hung on a nail outside the door to dry. PC Haigh, returning home from duty late one night, truncheon and lantern at the ready as usual, had an awful shock when he was confronted by a figure, swinging against the door.

As Hilda and younger sister Ella were sauntering up the garden path from school one afternoon a neighbour was knocking urgently at their front door. 'Mrs— is having another B-A-B-Y,' she announced. Flustered, their mother ushered them inside, then, spelling the word out, said to the bearer of the news, 'another B-A-B-Y?' Hilda and Ella couldn't help wondering about all this secrecy. After all, they did know how to spell. Why another baby from under a gooseberry bush should be such a closely guarded secret they could not understand.

If any girl had the misfortune to become a mother before marriage, all manner of unlikely lies were made up. If it had to be brought up by grandparents it was a major catastrophe, not because of the additional work, but because of the shame attached to the mother and child.

Children were too busy and happily occupied, helping in the house and garden or playing outside, to be concerned about how babies sprouted regularly from the gooseberry bushes. There were many far more interesting activities.

On a bit of rough grass the children's dad fastened thick ropes attached to a firm wooden seat on a sturdy tree for a swing. They took it in turns, willingly pushing smaller playmates on it. When the shrieks went up, 'oh, that's high enough', there was no question of frightening them, children were brought up to do as they were told and were happier for being obedient.

What could be better on a glorious summer afternoon than spreading an old tablecloth in the orchard, surrounded by the shade of apple and pear trees, redcurrant, raspberry and other bushes and foliage, and inviting friends to a picnic? A doll's teaset to drink the home-made ginger beer from, plenty of freshly baked bread, scones, pies and jam made by their mother. A tent, constructed from the upturned clothes horse with a sheet thrown over it, added to the Bohemian life.

After their repast the children lay on their backs and gazed up at the marvellous sky with fleecy clouds drifting by. Hilda could always see figures of people swirling around in those clouds. They watched ladybirds, butterflies and caterpillars lazily going about their summer lives. Or read story books and built 'houses', making a square room from stones or bricks lying around. Empty cotton reels made tables for any passing fairy, hide-and-seek was played among the trees and the thimble was hunted, all these activities combined to make an earthly Paradise.

Occasionally they ventured down to the beck, to dangle bare feet in the clear water, with many a stern warning from the open doorway of the cottage, 'Now mind you don't fall in'. If it was very hot they were allowed to have the tin bath outside, filling it with rainwater from the garden butt. It was so much easier to pretend than go to the seaside on a stuffy old train. Mud pies made in an old bucket, flying the old red, white and blue flag on top, were equally as good as the ones fashioned in sand. And all the children were agreed, they'd far rather find a fairy beneath one of the gooseberry bushes than a baby.

*The weir and bridge, Boroughbridge. These boys seem to be enjoying the water on this summer's day; Hilda, no doubt, was not allowed to swim here!*

## CHAPTER 7

# Barnaby Fair

A highlight of the year was Barnaby Fair which began on 11 June. Permission for this fair was granted in 1622 by Charles II and in the Charter was a clause, never to be revoked, permitting the townspeople to sell ale on Barnaby Day. All the schools were closed and many cautious householders barricaded their doors as horses were raced up and down the streets. It was rumoured that some of the more ruthless gipsies shoved a raw onion or stick of ginger up an old or ailing horse's rear end to make it go faster. There was always the benefit of lots of free manure for gardeners after this event had taken place.

*Jasmine Cottage is on the opposite side of this row of houses. Hilda was friends with the two little girls pictured in the garden on the right.*

There was as much excitement about this annual event as modern holidaymakers show about going to the other side of the world. The festivities lasted a fortnight. The first week was for the Horse Fair and the second week for the cattle. Sheep pens were put up by the Malt Shovel public house and stalls were grouped around the fountain up and up the High Street. Vendors from Sheffield converged on Boroughbridge, selling cutlery and pins. Extra police were drafted in as the fair folk gathered in tents and horse-drawn caravans, making their temporary homes in what was known as Gipsy Field. This was close to the beck which rippled along the bottom of the Haigh's back garden.

Idly swinging to and fro on the rope swing hanging from the big apple tree, Hilda loved to watch the colourful gipsies encamped nearby. In bed at night she used to peep out, hoping to catch a glimpse of the cavalcade of throbbing life, but usually nothing more than an empty field met her gaze.

Many a fight the gipsy lads and men had among themselves at the time of 'Barnaby Bright, Longest Day and Shortest Night'. It was quite a different matter from being safely at home being a spectator however, when the dark-skinned gipsy lads caught sight of Hilda and her school friends, Katie Lofthouse, Kathleen and Alice. They were chased all over the place, water thrown at them from mucky old tin cans. 'Still, if we'd been older, it might have been worse – they might have wanted to kiss us!' thought Hilda.

The gipsy caravans were beautifully kept inside. Often, on the long summer Barnaby evenings, the women were seen crocheting fancy edgings for their pillowslips. They also made pretty little pincushions stuffed with bran, which they sold to householders. Their menfolk, when not engaged in horse or cattle dealing, spent their time in the many pubs. Beer was cheap and potent, and whisky, before the First World War, was only about 4s 6d a bottle.

Lemon curd tarts were traditionally baked at Barnaby time. These were called Barnaby tarts. Many people entertained friends and relations, who visited the fair from nearby villages. Dozens of stalls sold luscious, curled, brandy snaps which were frequently given as 'fairings'. With a blob of fresh cream inside they were heavenly; or so my mother said.

Girls wore pretty summery dresses and big straw hats decked with flowers, with ribbons streaming out behind them. Their dresses were protected by the inevitable white pinafores when they set out to join the hurly-burly of the fair. There were swing-boats in the bottom square during the second week of Barnaby. Only the most daring girls – such as Hilda and Ella – ventured on them. Oh, how high they flew! Up to the sky then all the way down again, swooping like great, wooden, painted birds.

They loved the steam roundabouts too, and a glorious canter on one of the proud, painted Dobbins with their wildly flowing manes. This was all the gayer by the sound of the barrel organs playing music-hall songs. 'Oh! Oh! Antonio, he's gone away – left me on my own e o, all on my own e o, I'd like to meet him with his new sweetheart, then up will go Antonio — and his ice-cream cart.' These words were barely discernible midst all the hubbub and jolly clatter of music and voices. 'Down at the Old Bull and Bush' was another popular song that helped keep up the tempo of the fair, while 'Yankie Doodle Dandy' was ideal for riding round on those big, painted horses.

*A scene from Barnaby Fair in Boroughbridge, c. 1908.*

Before Hilda and Ella mounted their steeds, their father warned them, 'Wait till it stops, then I'll lift you down.' Their mother, dressed up to the nines in a black and white silk zebra-striped dress down to her ankles, topped with a huge picture hat swathed in the same material, that she had bought from the milliner, Miss West, was trembling with agitation as she waited for the horses to canter past again. She somehow feared that Mephistopheles might have snatched her precious daughters while they were out of sight, round the other side. The hissing of those old steam roundabouts was a constant background noise during the second week of Barnaby, from first thing in the morning till last thing at night.

Another great attraction was the row of 'Aunt Sallies' waiting to be knocked down. What grotesque faces they had! Hilda was relieved she had no real Aunt Sally who looked like one of those.

When their spending money was gone, the boys climbed up into the spreading trees to watch the goings-on. They fashioned arrows from bulrushes, sometimes targeting an unsuspecting merrymaker. More fun of the fair was to be had by pricking a hole in an old rubber ball, filling it with water from one of the horse troughs then squirting it into the crowds.

At other times a quiet, rural place, Boroughbridge honky-tonked to all manner of discordant notes in June. Snuffy Gin, that witch-like old woman, even added her strident voice to the general hubbub. Occasionally she even gave vent to a solo.

The sun is a shining to welcome the day,
Heigh-ho! come to the fair!
The folk are all singing so merry and gay,
Heigh-ho! come to the fair!
All the stalls on the green are as fine as can be,
With trinkets and tokens so pretty to see,
So its come, then, maidens and men,
To the fair in the pride of the morning.

Gipsies downed as much ale as they possible could, while local mole-catchers Dickie and Charlie, a pair of bachelor brothers, tried to catch the girls for a change. Even if the weather was boiling hot, Dickie and Charlie wore their usual stinking pairs of tight moleskin trousers and jackets, fashioned from moles they had skinned. Some said they probably slept in the outfits as well.

Years later, allotment holders who cultivated land where the old Barnaby Fair used to be held, sometimes found gold sovereigns in the ground. Hilda was never so lucky, but she was more than happy with the shining new sixpence that bought all kinds of delights. Even with no money, the gaiety of the fair was free for all.

*Boroughbridge in celebratory mood with bunting festooning the streets.*

# CHAPTER 8

# The Village Blacksmith

Barnaby Fair was one of the most exasperating times of the year for the village blacksmith. Gipsies often took a horse in to be attended to, then did their utmost to sneak off without paying for the work.

Born in 1902, Arthur Buck remembered his father being up at three in the morning to go to the brewery to fetch the horses. His first recollections were of sharpening heels and toes for horses before studs became the fashion, frost nails, and of when the forge used to be one of the 'brush houses' of Boroughbridge. A brush was hung out of the window to let the public know that beer could be bought there, for twopence a pint, during the day.

*Arthur Buck, the Boroughbridge blacksmith, in 1971.*

To learn the trade of a blacksmith, Arthur used to cycle to night school at Harrogate. These were rough rides, especially on dark winter evenings, with the lanes only dimly lit with gaslights, or not lit at all. Often, in the real old-fashioned winters of those days, he braved snowstorms in order to learn his trade.

He had to learn the anatomy of the horse from the knee downwards, then take the Registered Shoeing Smith examination. On the evenings when he didn't have to attend his classes, Arthur loved to play marbles with his chums beneath the gas lamp on Horsefair or play whip and top in springtime.

*The village blacksmith at home. A Bamforth postcard.*

Besides shoeing horses, much of the blacksmith's trade in the early years of the century was making the ironwork for governess carts. Trade was never slack as almost everyone had a horse: the brick yard, flour mill, butcher, coalman, corn mill, doctor, the brewery. PC Haigh didn't, he only had shanks's pony. The furnace at the forge used to be lit with straw and fanned by a pair of bellows which hung by the side of the huge open hearth. It was kept going with coal and breeze.

When Arthur Buck was older he enjoyed playing in the Brass Band British Legion, formerly the Town Band. He was a member for forty years, also a member of the council. As a boy, he could have all his tin 'boolers' free, as his father made them, selling them to the village children for a 'tanner' each. Arthur also remembered the wild Canadian horses during the First World War, and 'what rum 'uns they were'.

When motorized vehicles began to take over from horses, Arthur Buck made wrought-iron tables and similar articles. He also did a lot of work for the West Riding of Yorkshire, making tools and so on. But nowadays the forge, once the hub of village life, where people used to love to pause on wintery days to feel the heat from the glowing furnace, stands cold, empty and silent. But it is never forgotten.

# CHAPTER 9

# Home Remedies

While only a blacksmith was capable of shoeing a horse, ordinary people couldn't afford to enlist the aid of a doctor for every trifling complaint of their own. So most country folk relied on simple, trusted herbal remedies which one could gather freely from the hedgerows.

But eventualities such as appendicitis, if the sufferer's family couldn't afford to bring in the doctor, had to be left to take their course. This was often a fatal one. The King, Edward VII, was the first to be operated on for this condition.

Once, a cow died of anthrax in the village and its corpse was buried in a deep pit. A farm labourer dealing with the animal scratched his finger. Unperturbed, he slipped away to the privacy of a hedge where he urinated on the scratch and no harm befell him. The same treatment hardly sufficed another time when anthrax occurred. A local, John Willie, accidentally poured petrol over the cow's body in the pit, mistaking it for paraffin. His moustache and eyebrows were blown off.

If farm labourers cut themselves they slapped a wet cowclap onto the wound. Or, if none were nearby, a dock leaf was used. Urine was also considered a cure for chilblains. For the removal of warts, assistance was sought from white berries, known as candle berries. This was probably mistletoe. The juice was squeezed out and applied to the wart. Incidentally, mistletoe was never used to decorate a church lest frivolous encounters ensued.

In winter, when bronchial coughs abounded, brown paper smothered in goose fat, lard and mustard was applied to the wheezing thorax. As a preventative measure, the Haigh family thrived on lots of frumenty. This was wheat, boiled in milk, sweetened and spiced. Grandma vowed it would 'stick to the ribs' and keep out the cold. So, with frumenty within and oceans of goose fat without, the Haigh family seemed to withstand those real old-fashioned Christmas card winters of heavy snow, remarkably well. Especially when one considers there were only coal fires downstairs and stone hot-water bottles, or hot bricks wrapped in old flannel, in the beds upstairs. The absence of carpets and central heating probably contributed to the family's good health. But, as an extra precaution, a tin of wintergreen was kept in the house as well, to ward off winter's hazards.

During her adolescence, Hilda's mother looked into her eyes and pronounced her lacking in iron. So, she was regularly dosed with orange quinine wine and the red-hot poker was put to sizzle in a pot of Guinness to provide extra iron. 'Blood' and brain puddings, made from sheeps' heads, poor things, also featured in her diet.

The policeman's family's bowels were kept in top condition with Spanish juice. Always ready in a corner of the Yorkshire range was an old pot, cracked with age, with the motto 'If tha' does 'owt for nowt, allus do it for thissen' written on it. This was not to be taken literally in the Haigh household. Sticks of hard 'Spanish' were stood in the pot then boiling water was poured over them. After a while a thick black liquid was produced, strong enough to activate the most Constipated Being.

Brimstone and treacle were spooned into the children in the spring, to clear away winter's impurities. In the cupboard were plentiful supplies of Gregory powders to counteract feverishness. The weekly dosing of his offspring was a task assigned to their father. The village constable, used to catching criminals, had authority both outside and inside the home. Rounding up non cooperative youngsters for their weekly torment, however, proved a far more taxing job than chasing the minor wrongdoers of the locality.

California Syrup of Figs was worst. Spoon in hand, liquid dribbling all over the place, tripping up over pegged rugs during the chase was a sight to behold. It had been known for one unfortunate to be dosed twice by mistake, another escaping scot-free. Saturday was dosage day, so the children did have their ha'porth of sweets to counteract the awful tastes. A pink everlasting stick, tasting of peppermint, was best for camouflaging any lingering bitterness.

The constable had no rubber waterproof clothing so melted mutton fat was used to keep his boots waterproofed. Once a year his police cape was soaked in linseed oil to make that waterproof as well. Policemen needed protection from the elements, being out on the beat in all weathers. Only Inspectors, which Grandad later became, and Superintendents were allowed horses and traps for their work. Sergeants could have a bicycle, but the ordinary bobby on the beat was always on foot. They carried a paraffin lamp, hooked onto their belts, to light their way on dark nights.

If accidents occurred, the policeman was as likely to be called upon to give first aid as a doctor. At least the former didn't have to be paid and knew the basic rudiments. Once, a boy, playfully tormenting his little sister, was suddenly attacked by the enraged girl. She lunged a crotchet hook into his leg. Sergeant Foster was on hand, retrieved the hook, and work on the garment continued.

Parents had no worries about whether they should or shouldn't innoculate against whooping cough. In those days they didn't. Some concocted a syrup by boiling two ounces of the green herb called Mousear for ten minutes in a pint of water. It was then strained, and a pound of sugar or treacle added. This was given in frequent doses of a teaspoonful at a time; there were no side effects and with plenty of fresh air, wholesome unpolluted food and love, the majority survived.

Householders made use of their gardens for medicines as well as flowers. An ounce of raspberry leaves, with a pint of boiling water poured over them, was beneficial for sore throats. It also gave a speedy delivery with less pain, so it was said, if drunk regularly by pregnant women.

There were virtually no diseases that a home remedy could not either eradicate or give renewed health to the sufferer. Unfortunately, if cures were indeed affected, in the absence of the media, few found out about them. But 'old wives' tales' were certainly not to be sneered at, judging by the many successes and, unlike the present time, there weren't any side effects. Often the treatment given in modern times is even worse than the disease itself.

But back to simpler problems. PC Haigh was on his beat one day when he encountered a group of village lads who had been bird nesting. Charlie Benson had some eggs in his cap. How could he get rid of them when the familiar uniformed figure appeared on the scene?

Charlie had to act quickly. He swallowed the eggs. They were all addled. No one ever found out if a home remedy was needed for Charlie after that.

*George, one of Hilda's brothers, also followed his father into the police force. He is seen here (second on the right, hands behind his back), very smart in his uniform.*

# CHAPTER 10

# Scarlet Fever Hospital

No home remedy was effective against scarlet fever, endemic among children in the early years of the century. It was nearing the end of July 1910 and school was over for the summer holidays. It was a glorious summer of seemingly unending days of clear blue skies and glorious sunshine. But when life is perfect, sure enough, something happens to put a blight on the earthly Paradise.

The blight that summer was scarlet fever, which put nearly every schoolchild – including Hilda – into isolation hospital. Fever attacked Hilda after morning Sunday School. She only just managed to reach the back garden before being violently sick. However, she believed that was the worst part of her illness and over in those few minutes.

Even so, a horse-drawn ambulance cantered up to Jasmine Cottage shortly afterwards. Hilda refused to be carried out on a stretcher shrouded in the traditional scarlet-coloured blanket. She walked into the yellow van.

Her mother, weeping, Boroughbridge's drama queen as her husband always dubbed her, fussily buttoned Hilda's coat over her nightdress and pushed the biggest Jaffa orange she could find into her daughter's hand. Nonchalantly, for it was an adventure, Hilda threw the red blanket over her shoulders, assuming a superior air as she spied Eleanor Hall, who lived nearby, being carried into the van.

Importantly, the horse cantered off at top speed to the isolation hospital at Acomb. It left many Yorkshire puddings abandoned and flat that Sunday morning.

Nurse Beevers opened the door to allow air in as they drove along the country lanes. She must have been hot in her tight starched collar and cuffs, and ankle-length skirt. It turned out to be a splendid summer holiday for Hilda. Most of her school friends were already there. For those well enough, there were spacious lawns to play on. Nurse Rome soon made a favourite of Hilda, giving her gaily coloured ribbons and plaiting the child's black hair into pigtails or curling it with tissue-paper to make fat, glossy ringlets. Hilda enjoyed poking her fingers into them when there was nothing much else to do, and thinking how she would like to be a nurse when she grew up.

Truly they were in isolation, as visitors were few. When anyone did come they were only allowed to talk through a closed window. On one of those cloudless, sunny afternoons her mother appeared at the window, dangling a luscious bunch of plump, green grapes. Mrs Haigh had probably travelled by wagonette.

After a few tears were shed she fluttered her best white lace-edged handkerchief, while Hilda danced back to join the colony of fever victims playing on the sun-drenched lawns, and to share her grapes with any one who wished for a few.

Food was wholesome and plentiful. The thick slices of bread and dripping the children had for supper were especially delicious, honey-coloured, with a liberal sprinkling of salt. Lots of cocoa also had to be drunk.

Hilda had never been away from home for so long before, six weeks and two days, and she enjoyed every minute. It was like a timeless, never-ending summer idyll. Well, apart from the medicine and disinfectant bath on the last day.

Of a nervous and apprehensive disposition, Hilda began to think they had forgotten all about her as she lay in that steaming bath. It seemed to last for ages. Her vivid imagination conjured up all manner of possibilities – her skin peeling off, leaving her red raw, smelling for the rest of her days of that awful disinfectant and what if everybody else had fallen asleep outside in the hot sunshine?

Was she supposed to get out herself, or wait? Eventually she coughed away the timid frog in her throat and called out, 'Nurse Rome, Nurse Rome, I'm still here — .'

The nurse was one of those wonderful, reassuring people who, as soon as she bustled in with her beaming smile, set the whole world to rights. 'I just wanted to make absolutely sure that not one teeny, weeny, scarlet fever germ was still on my Hilda,' she said, patting her dry.

Not long afterwards her mother arrived with a wicker basket of freshly ironed clothes and Hilda dressed in the 'going home' room. Her mother told how the man had been to the cottage and stoved every single item. After not seeing any traffic for so long, even the sight of the horse-drawn wagonette made Hilda feel a bit nervous.

She didn't want to upset her mother, so kept to herself the memory of her idyllic summer holiday at Acomb. Six weeks of play, companionship, sunshine and blue skies in that little country isolation hospital. Yes, it was lovely for Hilda to be holding her mother's hand again, but oh, how she would miss her dear Nurse Rome.

# CHAPTER 11

# Whose Turn to Visit Aunt Louie?

A more normal summer holiday was when the question arose, 'Whose turn to visit Aunt Louie?'

Sarah Eleanor's sister Louie had married the proprietor of a fish and poultry business in Sunderland. Even though she was well off, and living in a house that seemed to the country constable's children like a mansion, Aunt Louie could not be expected to accommodate all of her sister's brood at once.

After being widowed, Louie continued to manage the business shrewdly and profitably. Hilda somehow sensed that her mother felt humble in her sister's presence. Her husband, when all was said and done, was only a village policeman. Aunt Louie was regarded as one akin to a High Priestess of Commerce. It may have been something to do with the manner in which she perched on a high buffet in her tiny, glass-panelled office in a corner of the shop. From this vantage point, she could keep a sharp eye on assistants and expected them to retain their pristine morning freshness all day long. They wore long blue and white aprons, topped with jaunty straw boaters. In jocular moments, Aunt Louie told her guests that the boaters were to stop hair falling into her assistant's eyes, causing them to give out too much change.

August saw the Haigh children eagerly watching for the postman striding up the little garden path. Would there be anything from Aunt Louie? Had she remembered who's turn it was for a holiday? She always sent the train fare in a registered envelope, making the postman's visit all the more exciting.

Until the scarlet fever episode Hilda had never been more than a couple of miles away from home, and then only on her bicycle. Her father had purchased the bike from the doctor, second-hand. Certainly she had never ridden on a train. No wonder she was terrified when the great, noisy, spluttering monster shuddered to a gasping stop, emitting clouds of steam, as she and her mama stood anxiously guarding their luggage on the platform.

It was Hilda's turn to visit Aunt Louie. 'You must be brave, Hilty,' said her mother, using her pet name for her daughter. 'Remember your father is a policeman.' But her nerve completely failed her when the Great Moment arrived to clamber up the high steps and a bewhiskered porter had to forcibly hoist the child on board. Once inescapably inside, her mother pushed her, clutching her doll, unceremoniously beneath a seat, taking the view that in such a low position the child would not be frightened with unfamiliar surroundings. On the opposite side Hilda saw sepia pictures of Highland cattle, shepherds and craggy mountains. As the train gathered speed, green fields of familiar countryside flashing out of sight, Hilda began to sob. Her Mama was in a highly volatile state of nerves herself and continued scolding the unhappy little creature for being frightened of, 'a simple bit of a thing like a train'. Anyone seated opposite could have been forgiven for thinking she was talking to herself, as no one else was on the seat.

Scared though she was, the sight of her Mama's shiny black boots had a comforting effect. Even though, above the creaking and clanging of the train, flowed her non-stop comments about Hilda's cowardly behaviour. 'A great big girl like you, I never heard the like of it. What will Aunt Louie think when we tell her?'

In between periods of this one-sided conversation, Mama, sniffling with feigned disgust, turned her attention to the passing scene in the manner of a seasoned traveller. But Hilda could hear her snapping her handbag open and shut, which indicated that she was more worked up than she pretended.

What drama as the train approached a tunnel, whistling and shrieking like a banshee! Sarah Eleanor whisked out a box of matches, striking them continuously until they emerged into the comforting daylight again. Seeing the light at the end of the tunnel was as close to a near death experience as they could expect before the real thing. But at the journey's end there was Aunt Louie and cousins, Nora and Teddy, waiting in a lovely big Hansom cab.

After the welcome, Hilda and her mother saw little of Aunt Louie. A stout lady with swollen legs, she rose early to prepare for the business of the day. Emily the maid had to wind yards and yards of bandages around her legs to support them for the long day ahead. Then Aunt Louie had breakfast alone, departing in a cab at seven. She always left a note for the cook about the day's meals.

Nora and Teddy were always given their 'salts' before breakfast. Shyly going into the huge dining room on the first morning, Hilda noticed Emily dispensing lovely fizzy drinks to her cousins. There weren't any for the visitors – the poor relations, Hilda thought. As Nora and Teddy threw back their heads to drain the sparkling mixture, Hilda slunk from the room. She ran to her mother, showering bitter tears upon her stays as she laboriously tried to lace up the garment.

'Emily is giving them fizzy drinks of lemonade,' she wailed. 'They get everything, just because they are rich and we are poor.' Never had she considered her family poor until that moment. Her Mama became more flustered than ever, even allowing 'Hilty' to tie the last pink lace of her corsets. An unheard of privilege hitherto.

Downstairs they went, in a high state of indignation. Emily explained that the 'salts' weren't lemonade, but Andrew's Liver Salts. Of *course* Hilda could have some too, and Emily even dropped an extra spoonful in to make it fizz more than ever. What a marvellous, bubbling sensation round her nose as, for the first time in her life, Hilda experienced a glass of Andrew's! She thought she would adore some before every meal, but Emily didn't think it a good idea.

Apart from that incident, holidays at Aunt Louie's followed a traditional pattern of joyous, summertime occasions. On fine sunny days – and there were so many of them – Emily packed cucumber, hard-boiled eggs and tomato sandwiches, and a jug of

*Hilda in Blackpool in about 1925. She is even fashionable on the back of a donkey.*

home-made lemonade for a picnic. Packed in a big wicker basket they took them to the beach. They spent long, golden hours playing, making sandcastles on Roecar shore, strolling through the park and reading Methodist magazines that Aunt Louie bought. Sometimes Nora and Teddy took a *Chatterbox Annual* and a book of fairy stories.

Other relatives were visited, such as Harold, who owned a hairdressing establishment. An opportunity to have their hair singed free of charge. How wonderful, thought Sarah Eleanor, to have a hairdressing cousin! After supper on singeing day Hilda loved to lie in bed and sniff the pungent ends of her hair, recalling, with a mixture of horror and glee, how Cousin Harold had to hastily apply a damp towel to her head, to prevent her black tresses going up in flames.

On those rare days when there was a fine drizzle of rain and they stayed indoors, Hilda was allowed the run of the bookcase. So many beautiful books, with lavish illustrations in many. *Bo-Peep* and Teddy's Sunday School prize, *The Life of Jesus*, a slim, gilt-edged volume with thin pages and many pictures of wavy-haired disciples and devout looking animals. But maybe the summer holiday treat she looked forward to the most was the apparently endless supply of sweet, cool, delicious home-made lemonade.

The evening meal, when Aunt Louie joined them in the stiffly furnished, formal dining room, was composed, as may have been expected, of the choicest fish. Throughout the years she never wearied of fish, which was served in many different ways at all main meals.

'It's my living,' she stated simply. 'It would be silly to leave any in the shop.' So plaice, halibut, Dover sole, herring, mackerel, salmon, all appeared in succession on different days. Fish, with lashings of parsley sauce, was the means by which they all managed to have a splendid summer holiday in their childhood.

## CHAPTER 12

# Willie, the 'Boy' at Ripley Castle

Having work one enjoyed was the main objective after leaving school. The butler at Ripley Castle was friendly with PC Haigh and when Hilda's elder brother Willie left school it was arranged that he would go there. He would live in and begin as the 'boy'.

When the day came for him to cycle off to Ripley, his mother wept as she packed some rosy apples from the orchard into his tin trunk which was going ahead with his few possessions by horse and cart. In it were a couple of freshly laundered shirts, white handkerchiefs, socks and copies of *The Marvel* and *The Union Jack*, bought with his Saturday pennies. No one knew when they'd see Willie again. In service, days off were a rarity and if anything cropped up at the castle, that took precedence over everything and the day off had to be foregone.

Poor Willie was homesick at first, crying every night for the first week, in his room over the stables. Compared with life at home, sometimes squashed three in a bed with his brothers, Alec, George and Ernest, being the 'boy' in a huge castle was a vast change.

There were so many people, including forty indoor servants. William had to work seven days a week, sixteen hours a day, more often than not. Boots and shoes had to be cleaned with blacking from a big bottle, knives and forks cleaned in a large round machine, and there were more dishes to wash than Willie had ever seen in his life. In frosty weather his hands sometimes bled after all that washing-up with soft soap and soda. The soap came in a barrel and had to be whisked to work up a lather.

When royalty visited, the gold plate was used. Willie had to wash all the silver too when it was returned from the dining room. Oh, what food and drink the gentry had! Sherry with the soup, claret with the next course, champagne for special guests. Servants knew when to refrain from filling glasses if guests began to appear a bit squiffy and the half-empty bottles later triumphantly turned up in the servant's dining hall. After the venison, roasts, savouries and desserts, finger-bowls were used, then the meal was rounded off with cigars and port.

*William Haigh, the 'boy' at Ripley Castle.*

*Ripley Castle where Willie Haigh started his career.*

In a slaughterhouse next to the castle laundry, animals were killed for castle food. Vegetables and salad stuffs grown in the grounds were fed with, as Willie said, 'hoss muck instead of chemicals'. The result was that the food he and everyone else ate, including the servants, was always 'top hole'.

Willie was measured for a suit of livery and sported a hat with a cockade for ceremonial occasions. He also wore long trousers for the first time and white shirts with bow-ties.

Willie's bedroom was next to Mr Wheelwright's and was reached by a twisting staircase over a gateway. Both rooms were above the stables. In wintertime the room was heated by a coke stove which stood on a flag in the middle of the room. This was lighted with a flint.

Huddled beneath the blankets, reading adventures of Sexton Blake, or another hero, by candlelight, Willie forgot his homesickness for a while until the voice of Mr Wheelwright boomed from next door, 'better put the candle out William m' boy or you'll be falling asleep and setting us all on fire'.

Then, in what seemed to be no time at all, the voice filtered through his dreams, 'time to get up William m' boy'. He daren't shut his eyes again, for it was his responsibility to rouse the butler, then set the table in the servants' hall.

At the close of that first anguished week, the butler, a kindly fellow, called the sad-looking lad to him and told Willie he could go home for the day.

It was a shrewd move. In comparison with the cottage, Ripley Castle seemed much more desirable. His tiny bedroom at home was positively claustrophobic. Long before the day was over Willie realized that he thoroughly enjoyed being the 'boy' at Ripley Castle. A boy with a huge bedroom all to himself and a chamberpot beneath the bed for his convenience alone. Then there was the pretty little 'Tweeny' maid he had caught throwing pebbles at his window to attract his attention, what fun it would be to pay her attention too . . .

In winter he had to struggle through great snowdrifts across to the servants' hall. There he had to pull a whacking great bell to summon them to breakfast, a bell that was heard for miles around. The first footman sat at one end of the table, the butler opposite.

On Sunday evenings Willie attended church, wearing uniform and a tall hat, before returning to the castle for further duties. He earned four gold sovereigns every quarter, plus three shillings and sixpence for beer and washing money. He had two smart uniforms, a bowler hat, a new pair of brown kid gloves every year and a blue mackintosh.

At Christmastide there were marvellous balls in the servants' quarters and a dance for the servants over at Nidd Hall. This was followed by an exchange visit from them. They were adept at entertaining themselves. Some played the melodeon and William (as he then preferred to be known), was a dab hand at playing the mouth organ.

Such lilting, tuneful, catchy music-hall songs, sung and whistled in that era made even working hard a joy. Willie had a favourite song, from the show *Our Miss Gibbs* called 'Moonstruck'.

I'm such a silly when the moon comes out;
I hardly seem to know what I'm about;
Skipping, hopping, never, never stopping,
I can't keep still, although I try.
I'm all a-quiver when the moonbeams glance;
That is the moment when I long to dance.
I can never close a sleepy eye,
When the moon comes creeping up the sky!

Then the romantic 'After the Ball is Over, after the break of day' and the rumbustious 'Ta-ra-ra-Boom-De-Ay', 'Soldiers of the King' and the swaggering, 'Man who Broke the Bank at Monte Carlo'.

When Willie's birthday came around workmates could not afford to give expensive presents, but what could a boy desire more than the Tweeny maid's promise of 'a nice big kiss', and a joyous singsong in the servants' hall.

# CHAPTER 13

# Easter

Meanwhile, with Willie and Hannah away from Jasmine Cottage in service, the rest of the family continued life in their happy, traditional way, with simple pleasures and religious festivals being the highlights of the year.

When Easter time approached, the village whipped itself into a hive of bustling activity. Every Thursday a wagonette, drawn by two horses, made the journey to Ripon market. The Haigh family helped fill it, for last minute shopping on Maundy Thursday.

The baker boy, who made his round between seven and eight on Good Friday morning, was hailed with delight. The hot cross buns were warm from the oven and they were eaten for breakfast, piled high with butter, fresh from the farm. After the family had been to church, fish was for lunch, of course, it being Friday. Sometimes, on the evening of Easter Saturday, there was the great treat of a magic lantern show in the village hall.

With the coming of spring, a tribe of gipsies made an encampment in the field and Hilda was able to lie in bed and see the red glow of their fires, and hear their joyful voices singing their own peculiar songs. Those swarthy-skinned women, wearing long, vividly coloured skirts, wore scarves knotted over their heads. Their washing was done in the beck that flowed between the field and the end of the Haigh's garden.

On Easter Sunday morning Hilda, Ella and their friends dashed down to the hen huts and gathered beautiful newly-laid eggs, still warm from the nests. Hilda sensed that the strutting cockerel and his harem knew it was a Very Special Day too, the way they kicked up the dust and crowed and clucked as though singing praises to the newly-risen Christ.

As she carefully placed the eggs in her wicker basket Hilda's heart almost burst with joy and Hallelujahs were sung in unison with the crowing of the birds. Who could fail but sing praises to a God capable of making all things bright and beautiful, especially lovely, speckled, oval delights such as eggs? Her mother coloured the eggs with cochineal or coffee and distributed some among neighbours. Hilda and her friends drew pictures on them; cat faces with long stiff whiskers, a yellow crocus, a daffodil or other simple adornments.

After breakfast was cleared away the family dressed in their Sunday best and went off down the narrow lane to church again. The small, grey, stone church looked beautiful all the time, but Hilda thought it especially enchanting at Eastertime. Daffodils proudly arrayed on window ledges brought a profusion of

*Boroughbridge church.*

sunshine to the somewhat gloomy interior and the whole Universe seemed to be throbbing with Easter hymns of praise, as the spring sunshine streamed in through the church windows. The 'toffs' sat up at the front of the church. Lady Lawson-Tancred, Doctor Daggett and other Sacred Beings. Ordinary families and servants always sat in the pews behind them.

There was a profusion of delightful hats, many bought from Miss West the milliner. Straw boaters, bonnets, flowers and ribbons all enhanced those contented, innocent, unmade-up faces. Sarah Eleanor considered girls who wore lipstick common. She herself was quite happy with Pond's Vanishing Cream and a few drops of lavender scent. Dainty lace, net and muslin jabots in delicate shades made heavy make-up unnecessary for the ordinary country woman. A simple style of dress suited their lifestyle and as long as a girl had a beguiling straw hat for Easter, she was happy.

Hilda's dad loved to sing in the old church and stood, straight as a ramrod, to swell the jubilant chorus of 'Jesus Christ is Risen Today', mixing up the number of hallelujahs in his enthusiasm.

As soon as the family were home again the girls had to change into an older dress while eating their midday meal. On Easter Sunday afternoon they strolled through the fields, picking wild primroses and violets, often following the route to the historic Devil's Arrows. The three huge stones, pointed like gigantic arrows, are a familiar landmark of Boroughbridge, rearing up above the fields on the fringe of the town. At one time there were four of them. The stones are buried six feet underground and rear to a height of between sixteen to twenty-two feet, varying from twenty-six to thirty-six tons in weight. They were erected, it has been assumed, by Neolithic man, sometime between 2,500 and 2,000 BC. Hilda, Ella and their friends simply regarded those wonders as part and parcel of their Easter Sunday afternoon walk.

*An interior view of Boroughbridge church.*

When darkness fell, a typical Sabbath evening followed. The cosy 'boudoir', lit by a paraffin lamp, was alive with chatter and music, of a sacred nature. The children's mother played the melodeon, all singing hymn after hymn with gusto. 'There is a green hill far away, without a city wall', Hilda always thought this meant the hill that she played on and 'paced' the Easter eggs down next morning.

Easter Monday morning dawned, usually clear and bright. The children carried their coloured eggs in baskets to the sloping field and had fun rolling the eggs up the slope then trying to catch them as they tumbled down. This was called 'pacing' the eggs. When they cracked they were shelled and a scrumptious picnic was enjoyed. Their wine was the fresh sparkling water that gurgled in the beck. If it turned out to be a wild and windy festival, the children played with windmills and balloons, whips and tops, or flew kites on the springy green turf. If the windmills broke they could always get another from the ragman next time he came round calling, 'rags, bottles, bones'.

The girls resembled pictures drawn by Kate Greenaway. With ringlets and pigtails flying, their ribbons slipped loose on the pell-mell descent down the steep field, pinafores ballooning in the wind. They embodied the very spirit of childhood, Eastertime and the coming of spring.

# CHAPTER 14

# In Shadow Pantomime Land

One of Hilda's friends, Dot, slept with her sisters Marie and Gertie. At their bedroom window was a light-coloured blind. The girls were often awake when the customers were turned out of the Black Bull public house. As soon as they heard the laughing and talking, the three sisters leapt from their bed to begin the Shadow Pantomime Show.

Clad in long flannelette nighties they glided dramatically across the blind, holding whatever came to hand. A boot, doll, even the chamber-pot was daringly held aloft, balanced on Dot's head to the accompaniment of hysterical giggles. They also made rabbit's ears, twitching their fingers to resemble the animal. Drinkers were so amused that they began looking up at the window to see if the Shadow Pantomime was performing. A candle and a night-light were all the illumination needed.

There was a big lawn at the back, ideal for playing on. 'Three Pins to see a Peep-Show', written on a large scrap of paper and stuck to the front door, announced another kind of entertainment. A plank of wood made a shelf and small Japanese dolls, holding parasols, had strings attached to their backs to make them into puppets. Anything thought interesting was placed on the shelf, to attract the hoped-for visitors. It was surprising what a lot of pins were accumulated. Children couldn't afford to pay money for those home-spun entertainments, but they could always take a few pins from mothers' pincushion. Producing these concerts and plays in the back garden was a creative and satisfying way of spending a summer holiday.

For rainy days there were scraps, ready-gummed pictures of animals, famous people or nursery rhyme figures to stick into scrapbooks. Tracing was another enjoyable pastime as well as painting the black and white illustrations in a *Chatterbox Annual*.

The friends weren't pretty ringlets and innocence all the time. Indeed, they were a somewhat macabre lot. A man who lived in the Gas House had a fit of coughing outside the yard doors one day, coughing so much that he broke a blood vessel and died. Those who went to look at the blood, lorded it over those who had missed seeing the grass stained crimson.

Poor dwarf Joe Petch was unaware of the fear he evoked as he sat in the doorway of his cottage, gazing out harmlessly on summer evenings. Children dared each other to walk past him, ever so slowly. But they always ended up running and screaming like banshees. Joe wondered what monster could be chasing them to make them behave so wildly.

Hilda, Dot and the others liked to build a 'house'. Any old stones or bricks lying around could be used and placed in a square to indicate the rooms. A Wintergreen (clothes horse), with an old sheet thrown over it, made an excellent tent in which to lie on one's tummy and read comics. A discarded beer barrel or butter barrel from the grocer's, with a plank across the middle, made an enviable see-saw. The same barrel could be taken to the top of a hill, the child could get inside it, then roll down the grassy slope.

A highlight of the year, although not as exciting as Christmas of course, was the Gala, when the children danced round the maypole at Aldborough. Each child held the end of a long gaily-coloured ribbon and wove it in and out, singing:

> Come lasses and lads, get leave of your dads
> And away to the Maypole hie.
> For every fair has a sweetheart there,
> And the fiddler's standing by.
> For Willy shall dance with Jane
> And Johnny has got his Joan,
> To trip it, trip it, trip it, trip it,
> Trip it up and down.

Sometimes friends linked arms and sauntered down the back lane to watch tallow candles being made for Mr Bacon to sell in his shop. Oh, how the tallow smelled! Yet it was fascinating to watch long rows of thick cotton being dipped in it until they were the correct thickness. There was always great conjecture should Doctor Daggett be seen dashing along in his dogcart. How many babies did he have in his black bag this time?

Everyone loved going to the magic lantern shows in the Public Hall, and even to the Band of Hope meetings that were held in the chapel. These were quite jolly affairs, as long as you promised to sign the pledge of temperance. Hilda and Ella once went, although they were churchgoers, and almost wished they hadn't when they were taught how to dance a hornpipe to the song, 'We'll may the Keel Row'. Ella was told she wasn't doing it right. She was most indignant. 'You're just saying that because we go to church and not chapel,' she protested. But she was 'talked round' and the intricate footwork eventually mastered, enough for her to dance blithely down the lane afterwards, showing off her new skill.

In that small community no one had to go far for anything to be attended to, everything was within walking distance. A clock to repair? 'Clocky' Taylor was a dab hand at that. Dot remembered a lady, Dolly Birkhill, who used to sell brandysnap. If a child hadn't any money, he or she was shooed away, Dolly calling out, 'Only a penny, honey, run away and ask your mammy for a penny.'

*The Devil's Arrows, Boroughbridge.*

Dot usually had a penny for brandysnap, but she never got over the disappointment she suffered one Christmas. A number of times her mamma had taken her to Miss Humpleby, a dressmaker, ostensibly because Dot was the same size as a little girl in Harrogate, who wanted a new dress made.

That Christmas Eve Dot hung her stocking over the fireguard in a fever of gleeful anticipation. She scrawled her name in big letters on a bit of paper and pinned it to the black woollen stocking. She had been hoping for a new doll for weeks.

So when, with trembling fingers, she opened a long box lying on her bed next morning and saw that it was a dress and not the longed-for doll, she could not refrain from weeping with uncontrollable disappointment. Even the selection box of various chocolate novelties, an orange and an apple, a box of picture building bricks, a mosaic game and beads to thread, could not appease her.

All children, whatever they found or did not find in their Christmas stockings, derived the same amount of pleasure from skating and sledging on the snow and ice that was there. How they longed for the canal to freeze over again during the Christmas holidays as it had done in 1891. The ice was so firm that locals could skate across it to the shops to do their shopping, carrying back laden baskets in perfect safety. A winter wonderland indeed.

Youngsters loved to play on the bridge over the River Tutt at the bottom of St Helena. This bridge was reputedly fashioned from one of the Devil's Arrows.

The story was that John Metcalfe, who lost his sight after smallpox, aged six, built the bridge. He became famous as a civil engineer, despite his disability. Known as Blind Jack of Knaresborough, he died in 1810, aged ninety-five.

Children never tired of hearing about the Devil, who, when attempting to destroy nearby Aldborough, took his stand on Howe Hill and hurled the famous huge stone arrows with the warning:

> Borobrigg keep out o'way
> For Aldborough Town
> I will ding down.

Some experts considered the standing monoliths of millstone grit to be the oldest in the country.

The mystic majesty of the arrows never failed to fire the imagination of Hilda, Dot, Katie and the others. In one of the stones was discovered a small hole. Greatly daring, the girls, one after the other, pushed a finger inside, ran round the stone three times, then watched, with beating hearts, for the Devil to come out of the top.

He never did. But there was always the chance that he might . . .

*A 'promotional' postcard for Boroughbridge showing all the places of interest and, of course, the famous Devil's Arrows.*

# CHAPTER 15

# Christmas Joys

Singing traditional songs and carols does a great deal to lift the spirits. Although there were no music lessons, apart from singing at school, how superb it was to be in a class roaring out, 'Men of Harlech', 'Tom Bowling', 'The Ash Grove' and 'Dashing Away with the Smoothing Iron'. Hilda wondered why she never saw any ladies running up the lanes with their flat-irons when there was a song about them. Hilda was also allowed to have piano lessons, sixpence an hour with the local piano teacher.

The little village school supplied everything else needed to equip the children for Life. The three 'Rs', courtesy, good manners, a respect for their elders, animals, and every living thing. 'I want' didn't come into the children's vocabulary. Instead, they may have prayed, hoped, and window-gazed in those exciting days before Christmas, or maybe written a letter to Santa Claus, beginning with a 'please' and many 'thank you's at the end.

Anticipation was frequently better than arrival. All could admire picture bricks and beautiful dolls with rosy-cheeked china faces, on which the candlelight cast its soft glow in dark December days. Time, however, was of more importance than money. Hilda and Ella had a long list of teachers, friends and relations for whom they intended to make presents, and the hours sped by all too rapidly.

Their father gave them old police books with clean, empty pages still left in them. After school, by the light of the oil lamp, they locked themselves in the tiny front room and set to work. Ella, being the youngest and most determined, insisted that *she* crayon the robins, plum puddings with sprigs of red-berried holly and angels on the front covers of their home-made notebooks. Hilda was relegated to the menial task of cutting pages into neat squares, folding them, then stitching them together down the centre.

The girls created the decorations for the house entirely from home-made or home-grown materials, or from anything suitable found lying around the house. Thick white cap paper, which the baker's errand boy wrapped bread in on the few times their mother 'wasn't feeling up to making it', was pounced upon with glee. In the Christmas workroom this was fashioned into row after row of paper angels, fat Chinese lanterns and crayoned paper 'fly' balls to hang from the dark brown picture moulding.

At Christmas time, shopkeepers usually presented customers with coloured candles, almanacks or a big box of biscuits with a lovely picture on the lid. Sometimes it was shortbread in a tartan wrapper with a black dog on the front wearing a tartan collar and bow-tie.

On the morning of Christmas Eve Hilda and Ella muffled themselves up, buttoned their gaiters, and rushed out into the frosty air to gather holly, mistletoe and other greenery from the lanes and fields. When dusk fell there was wassailing outside cottage, farm and homestead. Girls weren't allowed to go carol singing alone, in those days of no street lighting. So, Willie, George, Ernest and Alec accompanied them, carrying lanterns, until Willie left home to work at Ripley Castle. On their return they were ready for the traditional Christmas Eve meal of frumenty.

Their mother busied herself clipping the last pieces into the rug she had been pegging away at during the dark evenings. She kept the final clips back so there would be a present for the house on Christmas morning too. Happy hours were spent making up a pattern, matching or contrasting the bits of material out from old clothes. Weight and solidity were the watchwords in those days; didn't those rugs take some shaking!

One Christmas Eve, when Hilda was eight or nine and over-excited about what the morrow may bring, there was nearly a disaster. Her dad, still in his police uniform, was having a nap before the fire, stretched out on the horsehair sofa, breathing deeply. Sarah beckoned her daughter to take the lading can of hot water from the boiler. The 'piggin', as they used to call the lading can, was heavy, Hilda's hand was small, and her mind not fully on the job.

She was thinking about Santa Claus and wondering where he and his reindeer were at that moment. How far away was he from Jasmine Cottage? She was passing her reclining father when, somehow or other, the whole can, full of scalding hot water, spilled a few drops over PC Haigh's almost bald and unsuspecting head.

He shot up from his reclining position, rubbing his head. 'Blockhead, you blithering blockhead!' he exploded after his rude awakening.

Hilda flew off into the neighbouring fields, hearing in sheer misery the strains of 'Silent Night' and 'God Rest You, Merry Gentlemen', floating across from the brass band in the square. She didn't return until she was sure her father's head and temper would have cooled. Then, slinking indoors with a pathetic look on her face, she presented him with a home-made notebook with, 'For Dear Father' printed on the outside, a spill holder made from a tube of cardboard and decorated with coloured paper, and two ounces of his favourite 'baccy', all this much earlier than she intended. But 'blockhead' she remained for many days after.

Like most children on Christmas morning, the Haigh brood were delighted to find an apple, an orange, packets of nuts and raisins, a selection box – full of chocolate cigars and animal shapes – and a shiny new penny in their black woollen stockings. Hilda preferred stockings over her brass bed-rail to the pillowcases that some children boasted about. They looked so much more exciting with all the strange lumps jutting out. Sometimes there was a pretty bunch of hair ribbons, a handkerchief with her initials embroidered on or a little Japanese doll, the size of a clothes peg, with black wool for hair, a chalk-white face, and wearing a kimono made of crinkly purple and white flower-patterned paper.

*Another typical festive postcard. Hilda would no doubt have enjoyed similar snowfalls and dressed accordingly.*

One Christmas, Hilda was enchanted with a sky-blue enamel cooking stove, and a little set of cooking utensils in the stocking. Pretend Christmas puddings were baked many times that happy day. Another year the girls were thrilled to receive equipment for French knitting. This was only an empty cotton reel with four nails hammered into the corner, and a few balls of gaudy striped wool, but how their imaginations took off.

The cottage was soon enlivened with a riot of lumpy mats on which to stand vases of flowers, or jam jars when there weren't enough proper vases. The teapot had a new mat, a jazzy affair of vivid yellow, midnight blue, green and garish orange. Friends were given mats for Christmas, birthdays, or just any old time there was another one produced. How enjoyable it was to see who could pull the first bit of French knitting through the cotton reel on those cosy winter evenings round the fireside.

A day or two before Christmas was the Sunday school party. A huge pine tree, lit with tiny candles and decorated with shiny baubles and presents, dominated the Sunday School room, causing gasps of delight from the scholars. One year Hilda fell in love with a skating lady, made of tin who hung at the top of the tree. Her joy knew no bounds when it was given to her. There was a little key in the skating lady's side and after she was wound up, she skated gracefully over the oilcloth on the table. Care had to be taken in case she skated to her death over the side.

After the feasting, games of 'Pass the Parcel', 'King William', 'Musical Chairs' and carol singing round the piano, parents arrived to collect their children. It was an added bonus if snow was falling as they emerged into the December darkness, turning the landscape and cottages into a winter wonderland.

Sleep came fitfully on Christmas Eve itself, Hilda's dreams punctuated with visions of a red-robed figure clambering down the chimney. One memorable year she could wait no longer. She nudged Ella, snugly bedded down in the feather bed.

'D'you think he's been?' she whispered. 'I don't know,' replied a sleepy voice. 'You get out and have a look.' Having neither gas or candlelight, Hilda took some time burrowing down to the bottom of the bed. Yes, the stockings were no longer limp and there was a box sticking out of the top of one of them.

'Open it,' commanded her sister from the darkness. She did and what a clatter ensued! What a din! Enough to wake the dead or their mother and father next door. The noise seemed to go on forever as hard-boiled sweets rattled and rolled all over the uncarpeted bedroom floor, and scattered beneath the bed.

'What are you doing?' thundered their mother's voice. 'Get back into bed this very minute!' Hilda didn't need telling twice, for it was freezing cold. But two sweets were grabbed first, which she and Ella sucked beneath the blankets until they were small enough not to choke on if they fell asleep.

Church was first on Christmas morning, the different classes of people sitting in their own pews as usual. The Wilmot-Smiths from the Hall sat up at the front, their servants behind them wearing Sunday best. Men servants wore livery. No 'ordinary worshipper' left their pews until 'the gentry' had left first.

No one objected. It was reassuring to know there was a hierarchy of good, responsible people in charge of events. Besides, both Doctor Daggett and Doctor Sedgewick were good men, charging only what they thought their patients could afford. Irrespective of class, people respected each other, and behaved accordingly.

After the singing in the holly-decked church, the magical Christmas atmosphere spilled out into the open. Everyone was welcome in every home, to taste the Christmas cake and Wensleydale cheese, accompanied with a tot of ginger wine. In that close community, no one was forgotten or left out. Old, young, middle-aged, all worshipped the Christmas season together in complete harmony.

Great fun was had on Boxing Day when the men dressed up with straw round their legs and danced into houses, acting the fool and singing. The festive atmosphere was further heightened by an old man who loved to travel round the homesteads, from Advent to Christmas, playing the melodeon and forecasting the weather.

When the season was over, he went round the houses and cottages again to collect his presents. Hilda thought it wonderful, hearing his Christmas music on those dark nights when she lay snugly in bed, with all of Christmas – and life – still to come before her.

Many of the better-off gentlemen only wore tall, black, silk hats during Christmas, but the gentleman who kept the post office served his customers wearing his hat and frock coat every day of the year. Those in authority, however, always dressed in a dignified manner. No one can look up to somebody who is sloppily dressed. The Edwardian era was truly the *belle epoch* of English society, a golden era, with a God-fearing generation who kept the Sabbath sacrosanct.

On New Year's morning all the children marched to Aldborough Manor, where Mr Andrew Lawson-Tancred presented each child with a new penny. A policeman, sometimes PC Haigh, stood by to make sure that everything was done politely, and the children said, 'Thank you Sir'. The Hon. Mrs Lawson-Tancred went round the district in her carriage with a footman, giving out boots to boys and coats to girls who were known to be poor.

Crime was rare, but the Crown Hotel was broken into one Christmas. PC Haigh found the thief hiding in one of the big ovens, thankfully not in use by that time. Another Christmas morning, the crime was in his own home. Hilda and Ella must have been tired out because they didn't wake up until their mother was returning from early morning Communion. Disaster struck. Hilda found a pink sugar pig with a curly string tail in her stocking, while Ella was bitterly disappointed to have only a white one. So upset was she with her colourless pig that she banged Hilda's head against the brass bed-rail when her offer of an exchange was refused.

Sarah Eleanor, sedately walking along the lane from church heard the bang and ensuing screams as she neared Jasmine Cottage. Inside, her husband was called upon to administer law, order and justice.

With the wisdom of Solomon, he sawed the pigs in two, Ella received the head of her white one and a pink rear and, Hilda a pink head and a white rear. Peace on Earth, Goodwill to Men, reigned once more in the village constable's cottage that Christmas morning many long years ago.

# CHAPTER 16

# William, Footman at Brawith Hall

After his initial training at Ripley Castle, Willie moved on to Brawith Hall near Thirsk in North Yorkshire, as second footman to General Blythe, a retired Army officer.

At Brawith Willie had two suits of livery a year, dark blue with silver buttons, two red waistcoats, one bowler hat, and two suits for off-duty wear. Willie, aged seventeen, then earned £20 a year.

There was neither gas or electricity at Brawith Hall, which was some two-and-a-half miles from the main road. William's first task in a morning was to fill the forty or more lamps with paraffin, clean the glasses and polish the brass with specially prepared powder. After a hearty breakfast of bacon and eggs at eight a.m., in the company of the first footman and two chauffeurs, the windows and silver had to be cleaned. The male servants all lived in a cottage situated about two minutes walk from the Hall. The eight women servants, a cook-housekeeper, kitchen maids, and a lady's maid, lived separately.

Brawith Hall was a quiet, well-run country house. In October the family and servants moved to London for the winter, taking the silver and valuables with them. Luggage went by rail and the Daimler and Panhard cars were driven down by the chauffeurs. Living in London was like inhabiting another world for Willie, who, until a few years before, had never strayed further than the country villages near his birthplace.

The house in Park Lane overlooked Hyde Park. How Willie loved strolling to Speaker's Corner when he was off duty, to marvel at the oratory. Once, while listening spellbound, he felt a tentative tap on his shoulder. 'Well if it isn't Willie Haigh, all the way from Boroughbridge!' It was Mr Hunt, his former schoolmaster.

Going home to Yorkshire for a few days, one of the locals approached Willie, who was now quite a Somebody as he was living in London. 'Hey, Willie,' enquired the fellow, 'has ter ivver come across a chap called Smith i' London?' William, oozing metropolitan manners, courteously replied, 'I'm sorry, but I don't know many people there.'

No wonder. For when he knew that his son was bound for the Big City, PC Haigh had issued a stern warning. 'Now then, Willie m' lad, remember, only speak to policemen in London.' In those Edwardian days policemen were real worthies, all heavy beards and side-whiskers, bearing evil-looking truncheons.

Two years later Willie moved to his third place in service. This position was permanently in London, as footman to a Jewish family named Raphael, living at 38, Hill Street, Mayfair. They were very kind to their employees. Their own family consisted of three daughters and Cyril, who went to Eton. When Cyril was at home, he gave bundles of his 'old' clothing to William, who was allowed to send parcels home for his younger brothers. Even so, the clothes were a great improvement on the boys' best suits at home. One daughter often asked Willie to 'give me a piggyback' to the lift they had in the house.

Willie's parents made a memorable, once-in-a-lifetime visit to their London-based son. Mr Raphael pressed a gold sovereign into Willie's hand, 'show your mother and father the city, and buy them a meal,' he suggested.

By that time Willie was no longer the homesick, gauche young lad of Ripley Castle days. He was a tall, handsome young man with black wavy hair and a heavy moustache, stiffly waxed at both jet-black ends. He had acquired an elegant manner of speech too. The accent and mannerisms of the gentry tended to rub off on those who admired and lived with them. Indeed, Willie vowed he could always tell whether a girl was a servant or a shop, mill, or factory girl, because the former spoke so much better; with more refinement.

Every August the family and their entourage travelled to Scotland for the grouse shooting. A big, horse-drawn cab arrived to transport the servants to King's Cross station. Coaches were reserved on the train, and they travelled through the night, arriving in Aberdeen at half-past seven the next morning. Then they went on for breakfast at the Balmoral Hotel, before continuing the branch line to Alford, where petrol lorries transported them the seventeen miles to Castle Newe. The family and servants were in residence there for four months, the servants sleeping in a row of buildings called the Bothy.

Many shooting parties took place, while the ladies went for drives round Deeside. William (always William, never the abbreviated form when on duty) was tipped generously for the clothes he valeted for the gentlemen. Indeed, by the time the Great War began he had saved fifty pounds – a sizeable amount in those days.

Two or three times during the stay in Scotland, lorries came up from London to take the servants on trips to see the Highland Games. Twice during the season the servants were presented with a couple of brace of grouse to send to their families. They were occasionally given a blue hare as well.

Sometimes William went shooting on the moors with the gamekeeper. Other diversions were dances in the village hall at Strathdon. Traditional Scottish dances, barn dances and eightsome reels, to the accompaniment of an accordion and fiddle. Drinking in the dance hall wasn't the 'done thing', so the men hid bottles of whisky in surrounding trees. It cost sixpence – a tanner as it was then called – to attend the dances.

All were back in London in time for Christmas where William could count on more tips. These came especially from the well-to-do, fifty-ish lady who regularly visited the Raphael establishment. She rather liked the dark good looks of the family footman, calling William over to her carriage and pair before alighting. 'Are you well today William?' the lady always enquired solicitously.

Willie, then a debonair young fellow-me-lad who knew how to captivate the ladies, bowed courteously, a twinkle in his eye, and murmured, 'Thank you Madam, very well. And you?' Her Ladyship smiled graciously, slipping half a sovereign into the young footman's hand.

'I didn't need to attend a charm school to learn my etiquette,' he maintained. 'It simply grew on me when mixing with the aristocracy!'

Every Christmas Eve Willie had the pleasant duty of distributing the family's gifts to their servants. They received two gold sovereigns each.

Women, it seemed, were beginning to assert their rights and Willie was astonished to see some, suffragettes as he learned they called themselves, chained to railings. It wasn't money they were agitating for, but the right to vote. What was the world coming to? By May it was clear that the world everyone had known since Queen Victoria died in 1901, was going to alter. The Edwardian era was drawing to a close and, after nine years on the throne of England, the death of their King plunged the country into mourning.

*The funeral procession of King Edward. Who knows, Willie Haigh may have been among the crowds of people thronging through the London streets.*

Willie Haigh, who, until he went into service only knew about royalty from what he read in the newspapers, now actually queued in the streets of the capital to pay his own respects at the Lying in State of King Edward VII in Westminster Hall.

At the funeral, on 20 May 1910, Big Ben was heard tolling for the first time in history, reverberating over London, joined by the tolling of the great bell of the Abbey. It was that bell which first announced that Edward had breathed his last.

Spectators were rewarded for their long hours of waiting by the glittering troop of crowned monarchs. The sun blazed down and at ten minutes to ten, echoes of a single gun announced that the solemn procession had started to bear King Edward on his final journey.

Willie thought that, midst all the pomp and circumstances, one of the most pathetic sights was that of the King's

*A dignified portrait of the late King.*

favourite terrier, Caesar, following the gun carriage. Behind him came the late King's charger, with boots reversed, the saddle empty.

What a spectacle for the young man from the country, he had never thought such magnificence existed. The procession was led by bands of the Household Cavalry, their glittering sabres dazzling in the sun. There was a detachment of the Gentlemen-at-Arms in brilliant uniforms with nodding white plumes. The coffin was wrapped in the Royal Standard, over that was folded the gorgeous pall, gleaming with white and gold. On the pall stood the insignia of royalty, the crown of St Edward, the sceptre of justice, and the orb.

Willie stood in awe as the new king, George V, rode by on horseback, as did the German Emperor. They were followed by the Duke of Connaught, the King of Norway, the King of Greece, Kings of Spain and of Bulgaria, the King of Denmark, the King of the Belgians and the King of Portugal. The crowds also saw the royal princes, Prince Christian, Arthur of Connaught, the Duke of Teck, Duke of Fife, and others. The carriage of the widowed Queen Mother, Alexandra, was followed by the new Queen Mary, accompanied by the Queen of Norway and her children. After the royals rode Prince Tsai-tao of China and in the eighth carriage, the Hon. Theodore Roosevelt.

Thus Edward the Peacemaker was borne across the capital of his Empire, thronged with thousands of his weeping subjects. The procession continued to St George's Chapel where the King had been baptized, and where he had plighted his troth to Alexandra. It is here that Plantagenets, Tudors and Stuarts, 'sleep their long sleep until time itself shall be no more'.

Mr Asquith and Mr Balfour were in the uniforms of Masters of Trinity House, Mr Churchill, Lloyd George and Mr A. Chamberlain and other members of Parliament were attired in the dress of Privy Councillors. Eastern princes in their quaint costumes added a touch of picturesqueness to the scene, and the Dowager Empress of Russia walked into the chapel arm in arm with King George V.

Willie wished that he possessed a camera, he had never witnessed such a spectacle before in all his life. He was also longing to be able to listen to the service, but he could only read about it afterwards.

'I Know that my Redeemer Liveth' was followed by the 90th Psalm sung to a chant by Seltham, then 'His Body is Buried in Peace' sung to the music of Handel. As the bier descended gradually from the sight of the mourners, Westminster Hall was filled with the hymn, 'My God, My Father, While I Stray'.

Prayers were said, then a note of triumph was heard, a crash from a body of brass instruments standing at one corner of Westminster Hall, and the choir broke forth into song once more.

No great historical occasion is complete without the singing of Dr Watt's beautiful hymn, 'O God, Our Help in Ages Past'. The simple, dignified strains of

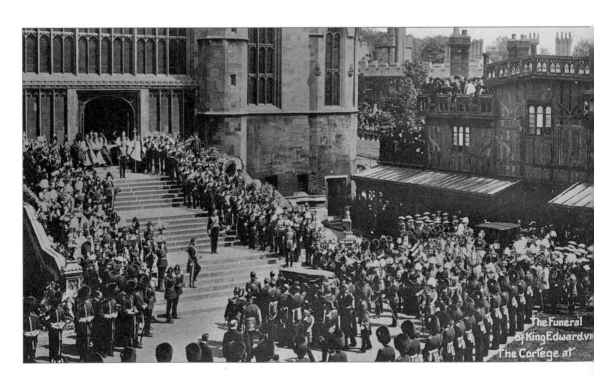

*The funeral cortège at Windsor Castle.*

William Croft's beautiful tune bringing with it a sense of hope for the future, and the feeling that we must all go forth to our work and to our labour until the evening, in the same spirit as that which animated our beloved Sovereign during the nine years of his all too brief reign.

The verses rendered without any accompaniment from the band were very pathetic and moving:

> A thousand ages in Thy sight
> Are like an evening gone,
> Short as the watch that ends the night
> Before the rising sun.
> Time, like an ever-rolling stream,
> Bears all its sons away,
> They fly, forgotten, as a dream
> Dies at the opening day.

Last of all came the intensely moving climax of the whole service. Commencing very softly, the touching strains of Orlando Gibbons's 'Threefold Amen' broke through the silence. As the voices rose and fell, 'a sense of nearness to the Divine Presence was borne in upon them, the balm descended upon all hearts, and a peace that passes all understanding brooded over the scene'.

The royal family knelt in prayer before slowly and sadly turning away and being conducted to the great doors of the hall. Thus ended 20 May 1910 and the spectators gradually departed.

> The tumult and the shouting dies;
> The captains and the Kings depart;
> Still stands Thine ancient sacrifice,
> An humble and a contrite heart.

The beautiful hymn, 'Now the Labourer's Task is O'er', another of the ones marking the funeral before the Benediction, was not applicable to Willie. He had to get down on his tasks again after watching the Biggest Spectacle of his life.

In London that May dressmakers advertised mourning wear. Ernest, of 185, Regent Street, had special arrangements to complete all orders in three days. Garrould's, in Edgeware Road, Hyde Park, had a large selection of 'Handsome Black Crêpe-de-Chine Blouses', the yokes handmade and priced at 13s 6d. They were also available in white and other mourning shades.

It would have been unthinkable to watch the King's cortège procession hatless (although gentlemen, naturally, took off their bowlers and top hats at the moment the late King passed by). A splendid hat for women, of black crinoline, trimmed with chiffon and chiffon rosettes, could be purchased at Garrould's for 12s 9 d.

Jet was also in favour. A black tunic, finished with an elegant jet fringe, the vest and sleevelets in fine tucked net, with a new turn-down collar and cuffs finished with jet sequin edging, cost 69s. For a wet day, what could be more appropriate than a Burberry, in grey or a dark colour, making a perfect mourning topcoat.

*A state portrait of King Edward and Queen Alexandra.*

Far more ladylike and elegant than wearing dark glasses to shield eyes from scrutiny at times of grief, was the fashion for black veiling over the face. Vanda, Court Milliner, at No. 30, Buckingham Palace Road, had impressive hats for sale. A Mourning Hat, in black crinoline, was trimmed with black Tosca net, with a long veil edged with lace draped over the back, hanging to the waist. It was priced at 35s 9d. Vanda also advertised the 'New Shepherdess Shape' in black crinoline. It had a flat trimming of black glacé ribbon with a half wreath of black silk roses, and cost 42s.

Many ladies still felt the need to embellish themselves glamorously, even in the midst of death. Hence the black curled coque feather boa, two yards long, from 15s 6d and 21s. A bereaved lady may prefer a black ostrich feather boa, priced between 29s 6d and 21 guineas. These were available in 1910 from Dickins and Jones Ltd, Regent Street. For the royal funeral that May, sunshades, especially designed for court and diplomatic mourning, were sold by Paquin, at 39 Dover Street.

But when all the outer show of pomp and ceremony is cast aside, the reportage in *The Queen* newspaper for ladies said it all.

'In the presence of Death, the great pale King, we men and women are dumb, for we know that all must travel by the same road and come, some swiftly and easily, some with slow steps of pain, to his great palace, whose gate is the gate of mystery, whose threshold the threshold of the unknown. He whom we mourn has passed through that gate and crossed that threshold; we who stay behind have yet to take the last road, but we may get a glimpse of it in that moment of clear sight which comes to us when we shut out the world and are alone with the dead. We know that our life is but a sleep and a forgetting, that, the veil of mortality torn down, we shall wake to a dawn of wonder. Death, after all, is not so terrible a King. The hand that rouses from sleep is no unfriendly hand.'

Just imagine, my Uncle Willie, with his heavy black moustache waxed more stiffly than ever at both ends, actually saw King Edward VII lying in state in that May of 1910. The event somehow touched both him and his family with a sense of being a part of the majesty of it all, a pride in being British, and part of the noble British Empire.

Meanwhile, the month before, on 28 April, up in Yorkshire, his sister Hannah had given birth to a baby, Winifred. Another brand new subject for the new King George V.

# CHAPTER 17

# Shops and Shopping

Kings may come and kings may go, but shopping goes on forever. Prices remained stable for a long time, and Hilda's mother was fond of an old saying, 'better go hungry to bed than rise in debt', a maxim most country people tried to follow. The family lived simply but contentedly, knowing not a penny was owed to any man.

Every week Hilda and Ella took the grocery order down to Mr Bacon, knowing that the goods would be delivered that afternoon. When they called to pay for them, the big, jolly grocer in his long white apron thanked them politely and then, as they were about to open the sneck of the door, called them back.

'Would you two young ladies care for a sweet?' he asked, and he gave them a big bag full of colourful boiled sweets. 'Now share and share alike Hilda and Ella' was his parting shot. One week Mr Bacon was more busy than usual. The girls' treat looked in danger of being forgotten – Hilda's eyes, large, hazel, and capable of great expression, gazed soulfully back as, empty-handed, they dawdled by the sneck. She flung a pathetic glance over her shoulder – it did the trick.

'Well, I never did!' exclaimed the kindly grocer. 'If I haven't forgotten your sweets.' He filled a paper bag and patted their heads. He was thanked effusively, and Hilda was so overcome by emotion that she even dropped him a curtsy.

Some novelettes and magazines advertised clothes on a shopping-through-the-post scheme. Mrs Haigh noticed an advertisement for a coney fur stole, long and straight with a luxurious muff to match. It was within her limited price range so, feeling pretty daring, she sent off for it. Then there were the days of excited waiting for the postman to deliver it. Occasionally she lent it to Hilda to wear for a walk after Sunday School, and the girl felt like a queen.

Sarah's large family made constant demands on her time, so she never had much inclination to visit clothes shops. But hats were a must, and Hilda used to ask the milliner if she might take a few hats 'on appro' for her mother. That way she could try them on in private, and, if suitable, send the money for the one selected and return the others.

Miss West knew what type to send for Mrs Haigh who, when she did manage to escape her domestic chores, liked to dress 'in a ladylike manner'. No outfit was more of a show-off than a mammoth black-and-white silk hat with black-and-white silk striped dress, reaching, as was the fashion, to her ankles. Everyone thought her very smart, but it was rather dazzling, and secretly Hilda thought her mother resembled a zebra in it.

*Outside the Black Bull pub, Boroughbridge, where Hilda used to get her mother's 'little drop of good'. PC Haigh is standing outside in this view, the taller of the two men in uniform with his hands by his sides.*

Although Sarah had never 'darkened the doors' of a public house, or smoked 'one of those common cigarettes', she did enjoy 'a drop of good' her euphemism for the word 'stout', with her supper. Her 'Lord and Master', as she jokingly called him, had to be well out sight up Roecliffe Lane on his beat before she furtively gave Hilda the tin can with lid attached. The child was despatched down the lane to the Black Bull where she tapped at the window where 'out sales' were dealt with. The landlady greeted her with a cheery smile. 'The usual, Hilda?' If any neighbours saw her, she was instructed to say the jug contained milk.

So Hilda was on tenterhooks waiting by that window, glancing round frequently to make sure nobody was looking. At times of emotional stress, a glass of stout was not strong enough to calm her mother's troubled breast. This happened especially during the First World War. She became overcome when Ernie came home on leave a few times; the sight of her handsome young son in khaki brought on 'one of her turns'.

The pain, Ernie knew full well, could only be assuaged by one medicine. Going for that medicine had to wait, however, until the constable was out of the cottage and out of sight. Then Ernie set off at a brisk trot with the small bottle to be filled with brandy, then only costing a shilling or thereabouts.

If his dad returned for something he'd forgotten before Ernie went in the cottage again, his mother looking out of the front window was the sign for him to hide the bottle beneath the peonies. If PC Haigh had ever found a bottle beneath the big clump of peonies, he might well have believed it had grown there, as his children believed babies grew beneath gooseberry bushes.

When a drop of brandy had 'bucked her up' Sarah held herself straight as a ramrod again and sighed, 'well, I do believe that medicine has made me feel better already'.

For a lady to go over the threshold of a public house, even with her husband, was deemed outrageous behaviour. No decent woman would dream of doing such a thing. Arthur William, as his wife always addressed him, wasn't interested in alcohol or public houses. A cup of spring water was good enough for him. He believed in setting a good example to his children at all times. His only extravagance was 'a bit o' baccy' for his pipe.

Hilda loved to roll the 'twist' between the palms of her hands, and sniff it before it was crammed into his old tobacco pouch. The scent of tobacco and pipe smoke was a reassuring reminder of his presence, even when he was not in the cottage. As were the row of pipes in a rack on the wall.

Winnie, like the older children, was brought up to watch her 'Ps and Qs'. Therefore, when she was old enough to be sent to the butcher's on her own and she had to ask for an amount of belly pork, skirt and kidney, she was in an awful dilemma. Certain words must never be breathed, and Winnie was sure her grandma had included belly in that list. And it was always petticoat, never 'skirt'.

However, she worked it out to her satisfaction before entering the shop. 'A pound of stomach pork, and a pound of petticoat and kidney,' Winnie demanded with all the assurance of an almost five-year old shopper. Her piety was laughed about for months afterwards by that surprised butcher.

## CHAPTER 18

# The Surprise

In April 1914 Winnie was four years old, and 'Mama' had to answer all the age-old questions again. Winnie did not ask how she was born, but why. That was easy, as by then Hannah's daughter had been enlisted into getting the weeds up with the other children on Saturday mornings. 'God wanted another little flower for his garden,' was the enigmatic reply.

After Easter it was time for her to go to school, and a white handkerchief was pinned to her starched pinafore. Her dress beneath had enormous leg-of-mutton sleeves. Hilda, then a 'big girl' in her last year at school, held Winnie's hand and guided her through the little lane. 'You'll be all right Winnie, you'll like being at school,' she encouraged her.

*Winnie Haigh in Blackpool in about 1925.*

A handkerchief safety-pinned to a pinafore was not much use if the owner had a bad cold, a pocket would have been better. However, a more serious illness awaited Winnie in October. Scarlet fever. Unlike when Hilda suffered from it, where she seemed to have the worst of it over almost as soon as the horse-drawn van collected her, the nurse accompanying Winnie to Acomb hospital voiced her doubts about the patient.

'I'll be surprised if this one recovers,' she murmured, and another voice said, 'she'll be lucky if she pulls through this.' To add to the drama it began to snow a little as the horse-drawn ambulance swayed over the cobbles on its way to Acomb Isolation Hospital. During her stay, Winnie pronounced doses of Scott's Emulsion almost as bad as her illness. But the nurses were kind and one imparted the startling news, 'you nearly went to live with Jesus Christ, Winnie'.

By this time she was recovering, and glad to put off going to live with Jesus Christ as her grandma, or 'Mama' as she called her, had promised a wonderful surprise when she went home. Something to look forward to, a surprise, often does the trick, swaying the odds in favour of recovery. Miracles can occur when there is hope for the future.

How well Hilda recalled poor Winnie's homecoming! Eyes glowing with renewed health, cheeks pink from weeks of fresh air and good food – most of all, the heightened excitement of The Surprise.

But first, her mama told her, she must wait until lighting-up time. Why, wondered the child, what was so special about lighting the oil lamp? A doll's pram with a new doll in it could be seen just as well in daylight.

As dusk fell Sarah, conscious of being the centre of attention ignored the oil lamp and began fiddling with two chains that dangled from the ceiling. Gas lighting, something Winnie had never seen before, had been installed during her illness.

'Now then,' beamed Mama, as the pale yellow light flickered round the room. 'What do you think of your surprise?'

Winnie was dumbfounded, almost to the point of a relapse. Surely this wasn't it? Her lower lip quivered and two tears slowly slithered down her face. 'I – I thought a doll's pram and a doll were to be my coming-home present,' she sobbed.

Her disappointment was understandable, although no such gifts had ever been mentioned. They wouldn't have been a surprise if they had.

What a difference gas lighting made, especially the gas ring where the water in the kettle could be boiled without waiting until a fire was lit for the first cup of tea of the day. But Hilda, who had harboured no alternative ideas, remembered the feeling of absolute wonder when gas was installed. How futuristic it was! How utterly daring! Those light, fragile mantles were like magic to Hilda. Light and feathery as a butterfly, liable to drop off like powdered rice-paper when finished. They had to make sure there was always a stock of them in the cottage.

Gas brackets were kept free of dust with a soft brush or duster, and when dirty had to be washed with a sponge wrung out with vinegar and water. They were then dried with a soft cloth and polished with a chamois leather.

What manipulations there were with the two central chains dangling from the ceiling. They had to be adjusted so carefully to achieve a proper glow. In fact, the family were all secretly rather in awe of them, and a teeny bit afraid of this wonderful new method of lighting. Especially if their dad happened to be on duty at lighting-up time, and the delicate operation was left to their agitated Mama. She was more used to the oil lamp, trimming the wicks and cleaning the glass shade.

Winnie could never recall feeling as deeply disappointed about anything as she did when she found out that the Big Surprise was only a horrible thing called gas lighting.

But before they had gas lighting, on cold winter mornings especially, it was awful for the first one out of bed, exchanging snug feather eiderdowns for the sharp contact of the cold, uncarpeted outside world. Those going to work, frequently went without a hot drink if there wasn't time for the fire to get going enough to heat the water in the old, black kettle.

Householders had to be sparing with water, as every drop had to be brought from the village pump, apart from when it rained and the water collected in a couple of huge, iron-rimmed rain tubs outside the back door. In summertime a small wooden table stood in the back garden, and Hilda loved to wash her face in fresh rain water. This enhanced a girl's complexion far more than any artificial means of make-up, which in any case was thought common by Mama. She had a tin of Snowfire cream and a jar of Vaseline to smear on her eyelashes, also a little bottle of lavender water. That was quite sufficient for anyone, thought Mrs Haigh.

But long hot summers meant that the tubs were almost empty so the children had to take buckets down to the fountain pump in the middle of the cobbled square. How heavy the buckets were, carrying them up New Row and trying not to spill a drop. Sometimes Hilda and Ella wagered their Saturday halfpenny that they could reach home without spilling any of the precious cargo. Not paying up if a spill did occur of course, that went without saying.

Then came the day when they actually had water laid on in the house. What excitement! But, like all new innovations, the novelty soon wore off. And my mother always said she wouldn't have swapped her childhood days for today. For, with all its inconvenience, the simple life generated plenty of work and thus contentment. The unfolding magic of each new day, with nature renewing itself, is full of surprises that far outstrips the delight of a new doll's pram – or even gas lighting!

# CHAPTER 19

# The Girls' Friendly Society

Winnie never did have a proper doll's pram, but she did have all the delights of a country child. Later, when she was able to ride a bicycle, she was entrusted to take sandwiches, in a basket hanging from the handlebars, with a billycan of tea for 'Dad' as she called Arthur William. In summertime he leaned against a hedgerow to enjoy his midday snack. The tea had cooled considerably by the time Winnie delivered it, but it still tasted like nectar in those idyllic surroundings.

She had no fears as she cycled along the narrow lanes, unlike Hilda, who was absolutely terrified of the dark and all its terrors, real or imaginary. Hilda used to go to the Girls' Friendly Society at the Vicarage every Wednesday evening. Her Mama's hysterical behaviour on dark nights, if any of her brood had to venture outside the safety of Jasmine Cottage, only served to heighten Hilda's dread. After umpteen dire warnings 'Hiltie' at last reached the door sneck.

'Have you got the hat pin?' her mama wanted to know, the weapon that was kept behind her lapel in case of attack. Then Mama put the pepper pot into her daughter's coat pocket, also to use if necessary.

The hands of the clock moved on, it was time to go. Sarah Eleanor stood on the doorstep, calling out reassurances, 'Mama is here,' as Hilda raced down the silent lane. Panting up the Vicarage path, overhung with trees and shrubs, where *anything* could leap out at an unsuspecting – or, indeed, suspecting victim – she thanked God that she had arrived, and prayed that the return home be similarly uneventful.

The Vicar's wife, Mrs Bingham, was a sweet, gentle soul who had charge of fifteen or sixteen adolescent girls on those Wednesday evenings during the Great War. They met in the Vicarage to sew garments, pillowslips and other necessities which were then given to charities. They also did knitting for the soldiers.

Once, Hilda made a straight magyar nightdress – anything more complicated would have been completely beyond her – and as she sewed she wondered what poor, destitute lady might one night wear the laboriously put-together pieces. She hoped the stitches would hold firm!

Mrs Bingham always wore black, relieved with a heliotrope coloured or white modesty vest tucked in the neckline. The dress sleeves were bulbous at the top, tapering to tightly fitting cuffs. The skirt was full and floor length. Soft, greying

*The vicarage, Boroughbridge, where the Girls' Friendly Society used to meet. The dark foliage that Hilda feared so much can be seen to full advantage here.*

hair was combed smoothly back from a centre parting, then caught up in a bun at the nape of her neck. Permanent waving had no place among decently brought up ladies at that time.

Inside the vicarage it was comfortable and cosy. There was always a bright coal fire, the girls sitting on high-backed wooden chairs and stools round the long wooden table. Slouching was almost a sin – how could a girl work, slopping about in an easy chair? Work was kept in a big chest of drawers, the girls' names written on scraps of paper and pinned to the individual pieces. Each Wednesday they always seemed slightly grubbier than the previous week.

As they had to walk past the churchyard to reach the Girls' Friendly Society a few friends met up along the way. What if some long-dead Boroughbridge ghost rose up and clutched one of them to its icy bosom? A terrible fate to be related to future generations of young children. Hilda could well imagine the scene in future years, the awful end of Hilda Haigh, 'the Bobby's lass', while on her innocent way to a meeting of the G.F.S.

The meeting began with a short prayer, blessing all who had attended. Then the friendly, helping hour sped by all too soon. Mrs Bingham cheerfully answered queries, taught the girls the art of home dressmaking and how to knit on four needles. As the hands of the clock moved round to eight, their dear teacher asked all her young workers to stand up straight and sing a hymn before leaving.

A favourite was 'Fight the Good Fight With all Thy Might'. If they couldn't fight as soldiers, they could at least play their part in the fight against evil, and do all they could to give comforts to those who were at the Front.

To each member Mrs Bingham had a kindly word of farewell. 'Thank you so much for coming my dear', 'I do hope to see you next week' and to them all, 'Now please on no account venture out if the weather is too inclement next Wednesday.' Finally, 'God Bless you all.'

When her companions had gone their various ways, Hilda raced towards the glimmer of the oil lamp which flickered encouragingly from their cottage window. Her Mama could be relied upon to be on the look out for her 'Hiltie', anxiously waiting for the familiar, slim figure as various shadowy forms loomed out of the darkness. As her boots clattered up the garden path her mama uttered a piercing cry, 'Is that you, Hiltie?' Had she not replied immediately the door would have been slammed shut and bolted again.

Both mother and daughter heaved huge sighs of relief when safely back inside the snug little cottage. Hilda's mama made an extra fuss of her, so thankful was she that no straying horse or other beast had trampled her darling underfoot, or perhaps a tramp may have kidnapped her child to be his slave in a barn or outbuilding!

How extra reassuring was the hot cocoa and oatmeal biscuits once the black, black night was shut out! Yet Hilda was always apprehensive when her Dad was on duty from ten p.m. until two a.m. She tried to force herself to stay awake until she heard the sound of his footfall on the garden path. From out of fitful dreams one night she saw the tall, gaunt figure appear in the bedroom doorway with lighted candle in a holder – still wearing his helmet – though his tunic was off and braces hanging loose in anticipation of a good night's rest. Roused from her sleep Hilda decided she needed to go outside to the privvy.

'Ay me lass, this is a bit of a nuisance,' he said good naturedly. They stumbled downstairs by the wavering light of the candle, making their way to the bottom of the garden and the Haven of Relief. PC Haigh stood on guard outside, holding the flickering candle, until his daughter emerged, shivering with cold. He flung his big police cape over her shoulders.

Warmly tucked up in bed again, the patchwork quilt rearranged around her, father and daughter kissed goodnight – Hilda feeling the stiff points of the waxed moustache brushing gently against her face. And so to sleep at last.

Some nights were disturbed when Mama affected a weak heart and indigestion, commonly known as 'wind'. Bellowing noises from her mother's bedroom, not unlike the utterances of the farmer's cows at milking time, woke Hilda up in fright.

'Are you alright, Mama dear?' she called out softly, so as not to wake the others. If there was only another deep bellow in response, Hilda felt her way tentatively out of bed and to her mother's side. She would find her erect against the bolster and pillows, her buxom figure in a flannelette nightdress, the picture of misery as she clutched at her heart, or where she imagined it to be. A big soda water syphon bottle was on the pedestal by the bed, alongside the little novelette she had been reading.

'All I hope is that I live until you're all old enough to take care of yourselves,' she moaned. 'I should never rest in my grave if I thought anyone was treating you badly.'

Then, as directed, Hilda rubbed between her mother's shoulder blades to try and dislodge the 'wind'. She privately wondered if it had anything to do with the 'little drop of good' that she had enjoyed before bedtime from the jug full of stout brought hidden beneath a shawl from the Black Bull.

Gradually, the discordant music and melodrama subsided. Then Mama altered her tune with a brisk, 'off back to bed Hilda, time you were in dreamland'. A few sips of soda water seemed always to do the trick.

Back in her feather bed, Hilda's mind ranged over the uncertain future. She pictured her Mama, lying beneath six feet of earth, tossing, turning, and bellowing pitifully in her grave. Where no one could reach her ever again to rub between her shoulder blades and give relief.

Then, salvation! All nightmares vanished at the sound of her Dad turning his key in the lock, his boots being thrown onto the kitchen floor. 'Arthur William, is that you?' Mama's voice floating on the black night air. The answer was in the affirmative, 'Yes, hinny, I'm home.' His wife being from Sunderland, he called her 'honey' with the Northern pronunciation.

Suddenly, all was right with the world. All the awful thoughts disappeared, and bed was once again a safe, warm, sanctuary for body and mind. But before slumber claimed her finally, one member of the Girls' Friendly Society was pictured in her mind's eye. Dolly, the Vicar's daughter, a tomboy, who was usually clad in brogues and tweeds, in bed at the Vicarage. What did she look like when asleep Hilda mused, did Dolly wear a nightdress, or pyjamas?

Oh well, only another seven days and then it would be Wednesday again. Hilda was not much good as a seamstress and preferred 'titivating' hats to the intricate business of cutting out dress patterns and knitting Balaclavas and khaki gloves on four needles. However, it was wonderful to recall the friendly faces, lovely hymns and cordial atmosphere which helped even Hilda succeed in making a passable garment for someone in need.

Soon it would be time for Mr Bruce, the milkman, bearded and side-whiskered, to make his first round of the day. Mr Bruce wore a cream-coloured smock, and the sound of his milk churns rattling over the cobbles when daylight returned was very reassuring.

Even though England was at war with Germany, summer would come round again, and Hilda would be able to saunter through the lane to the Vicarage, with no fear of ghosts or other fiends of the night. Milk would have to be kept in jugs of cold water down in the cellar to stop it turning sour in the heat – the umpteen scones that had to be baked when it did, so as not to waste the milk! But in wintertime the oven shelves had pieces of old worn blanket wrapped round them before being placed in beds, to stave off the chill.

With such thoughts Hilda again thanked God for Mrs Bingham and the Girls' Friendly Society. Their welcome always made her feel as though she'd been away for years, maybe to the North Pole, or taking on the Kaiser single-handed, rather than a mere short sprint up the village street.

Yes, the bilious bouts of her Mama notwithstanding, life was good and soon she would know who had won the Empire Day prize on Citizenship, and the light nights would be here again.

# CHAPTER 20

# The Empire Day Prize

Hilda prided herself on correct spelling and being able to tell a good story. It was a challenge, when, in 1915, and in her last year at Boroughbridge school, the competition for that year's Empire Day book prize essay was on the subject of 'Citizenship'. The competition had been devised by Mr B.T. Hutton-Croft, of Aldborough Hall.

Then aged fourteen, it was Hilda's third attempt at the Empire Day prize. Brought up on the maxim, 'if at first you don't succeed, try, try, try again', she did so. As with many joys of life, the attempting, the striving, the doing one's best, even if one does not win the longed-for prize, 'keeps you on your toes', her mother always told her.

Patriotism was the order of the day. The Union Jack flag, the old red, white and blue, sent a surge of pride in being British through Hilda and her school fellows when 24 May, Empire Day, arrived. How she revelled in singing the old stirring songs as they marched round, waving their individual Union Jacks! The pianist in the schoolroom loved the occasion every bit as much as those fervent scholars. They began with 'The Ash Grove'.

*Aldborough Hall, the home of Mr B.T. Hutton-Croft, who presided over the Empire Day celebrations.*

> Down yonder green valley, where streamlets meander,
> When twilight is fading I pensively rove;
> Or at the bright noontide in solitude wander,
> Amid the dark shades of the lonely Ash Grove.

But Empire Day was far from morbid, unlike the outcome of this particular song. In the early part of the Great War girls and boys thrilled to the march of the 'Men of Harlech'.

> Men of Harlech, in the hollow,
> Do ye hear like rushing billow,
> Wave on wave that surging follow,
> Battle's distant sound?
> 'Tis the tramp of Saxon foemen
> Saxon spearmen, Saxon bowmen,
> Be they knights, or hinds, or yeomen,
> They shall bite the ground!

Added poignancy, determination and full-throated patriotism were all the more vibrant that first Empire Day of the Great War as many of the singers' brothers were away from home already, 'fighting the Hun'. It was as if the very fervour of their songs could help those beloved brothers fight and win the war. Hilda's brother Ernie was now one of those 'lads in khaki'.

There were other topics to sing about and praise as well though. 'The Roast Beef of Old England' was sung to a tune by R. Leveridge, dating from about 1728. The pianist certainly agreed to the instructions on her sheet music, 'with spirit'.

> When mighty roast beef was the Englishman's food,
> It enobled our hearts, and enriched our blood,
> Our soldiers were brave and our courtiers were good.
> (REFRAIN) Oh! the roast beef of old England!
> And oh! for old England's roast beef.

On this special day the girls wore their starched white pinafores, contrasting with their red, white and blue flags. Long hair was in shining, be-ribboned ringlets, pigtails, or simply straight flowing locks. Local dignitaries solemnly watched the proceedings from their appointed places on the school platform, clad in dark suits and white shirts with stiff collars, cuffs, cufflinks, and highly polished black boots or shoes. A look of importance was on every face.

Behind each eye there was probably a hint of nostalgia, a yearning, to be in the 'front line' of action, as there most likely was with the schoolboys who bellowed out, 'The British Grenadiers'.

> Some talk of Alexander, and some of Hercules,
> Of Hector, and Lysander, and such great names as these,
> But of all the world's great heroes, there's none that can compare,
> With a tow, row, row, row, row, row, row, to the British Grenadiers.

None wanted the morning's celebrations to end, it was all so exhilarating. One of the girls, who had a sweet soprano voice, sang 'Cherry Ripe'. 'Cherry ripe! Cherry ripe! ripe, I cry, Full and fair ones, Come and buy, Cherry ripe, cherry ripe, ripe, I cry, Full and fair ones, Come and buy.' Like the cherry on top of a bun, put aside on the plate as a treat for the very last, Hilda half longed and half dreaded for the songs and choruses to be over so the name of the prize winner would be announced. Had she won or hadn't she? Certainly she had done her very, very best when writing her essay . . .

But the songs weren't over yet. 'Now is the month of Maying, When merry lads are playing, Fa la la la la' (oh goodness, how many more fa la las?) Then they had to include a few rousing sea shanties, 'The Bay of Biscay' – enough to make anyone see sick simply singing about it – and 'Land of My Fathers', a tribute to Wales. Ireland mustn't be forgotten, so 'Killarney' followed on, then 'The Bluebells of Scotland'.

> Oh where, and oh where, is your Highland laddie gone,
> Oh where, and oh where, is your Highland laddie gone?
> He's gone to fight the foe for King George upon the throne
> And it's oh! in my heart, I wish him safe at home.

The very thought of that poor Highland laddie and her brother Ernie, may be at that very moment facing bayonet, shell and gunfire, was almost too much to bear for Hilda. All this along with the knowledge that soon, very soon, the announcement would be made of who was the winner of that year's Empire Day Prize. Her heart was thumping beneath her starched pinafore, almost enough to burst.

She scanned the faces of the bigwigs on the platform, including that of the Vicar, the Revd Bingham. All were serenely impassive, not one looking in her direction – oh, if only she knew!

Then, rather slowly, too slowly for Hilda's state of mind, the pianist urged all to join in, 'The Minstrel Boy to the war has gone, In the ranks of death you'll find him.' (Hilda dabbed her eyes with her spotless white handkerchief, quite unable to continue. 'His father's sword he has girded on, And his wild harp slung behind him.' (Oh Ernie, Ernie, will you ever hide the brandy bottle among the peonies again?) 'Land of song, said the warrior bard, Tho' all the world betrays thee, One sword at least thy rights shall guard, One faithful harp shall praise thee.'

The morning, however, was getting on but, 'We can't let Empire Day go by without all singing "The Dear Little Shamrock" can we?' the teacher asked. 'No!' roared the children delightedly. The pianist struck up again, then they *must* have 'Heart of Oak' yelled one of the boys. The chorus just about raised the rafters, all imagining themselves at sea, heroes, one and all.

> Heart of oak are our ships, heart of oak are our men,
> We always are ready, steady, boys, steady!
> We'll fight and we'll conquer again and again.

Hilda was fourteen now, and would have to leave school soon. No more opportunities would come her way to win that coveted Empire Day Prize, and it was the best feeling of all to be a hero, or heroine, even the winner of a prize.

The piano stopped playing, the voices were hushed. A few elderly gentlemen on the platform coughed, clearing their throats for the next important part of the proceedings. A hush fell over the assembled throng and a palpable air of expectation filled that May morning.

The vicar thanked the boys and girls, and the pianist, for such a rousing start to Empire Day. What are songs such as those if not sung with pride and gusto? The school had done justice to them. May children of the future still sing them with pride. There was a prayer, for 'our lads' serving King and Country and thanks to those who had decorated the school with garlands of red, white and blue, bunting outside and inside, and the enormous Union Jacks either side of the platform.

'But now,' he continued, 'I won't keep those of you who wrote such marvellous essays, on the subject of Citizenship, in suspense any longer . . . .' Another deliberate wait, nervous giggles ran like lightning through the competitors, each trying to appear as though the last thing in the world they expected was to be announced the winner.

Before being seated again, the Rev. Bingham addressed Mr B. Hutton-Croft, of Aldborough Manor, 'Who I will now ask to announce the name of the winning essay.'

Up rose The Important Man. 'Before I do that, may I just remark on the content of that essay; the writer referred to the history of Canada, the geographical subject of this year, its annexation to the British Empire, and the great responses made by her people to assist the Mother Country in her present stupendous struggle both in men and provisions.'

Hilda felt as though she was about to faint – but she'd never fainted before and didn't know how to do it – those words were hers, surely somebody else hadn't written the same? Suddenly she felt that all the preparations, the flags, the songs, that Empire Day itself, on this one occasion, came secondary in importance to being the prizewinner.

Mr B. Hutton-Croft continued, 'the young lady's essay on citizenship has brought out the duty of British citizens to be patriotic, sympathetic, and industrious.' A few more parts of Hilda's composition were quoted. She had emphasized the power of discipline, in the story of the loss of the *Birkenhead*. The freedom enjoyed by Britons had been touched upon, and the formation of good habits while young cited as a means of producing good citizens. (Being a member of the Girls' Friendly Society had inspired that bit.)

Mr Hutton-Croft noted that there were still a couple of songs to be played, but he really mustn't keep the winner in suspense one moment longer. 'And the winner of this year's Empire Day essay is . . . Hilda Margaret Haigh! Give her a clap everybody – come up here Hilda, well done!' Trembling with pride and the release of tension, my mother, as she would become, went forward to shake hands with all those august personages on that beautiful May morning.

The prize, *Our Empire Story*, a lovely big book with a dark blue cover had a crown and Union Jack surrounded with laurel leaves on the front. Inscribed inside were the words, 'For Hilda Haigh from B. Hutton-Croft on the occasion of her winning the Empire Prize Essay, Empire Day, 1915. The donor hopes that the Winner will never forget how patriotically the Colonies have supported the Mother Country in her greatest war.'

There were some thrilling-looking coloured plates along with the stories, with captions such as, 'These cruel men meant to turn Hudson adrift on the Icy waters' and 'Alone across the Trackless Snow'. There was another picture of a raft, men with guns, and Indians, captioned, 'No man was safe, no life was sure.' There was lots more to look at, but now was not the time to keep turning the pages. Hilda was invited to remain on the platform until the close of the celebrations. She also received £5, to put in the post office until she was eighteen.

The vicar rose to his feet again. He went on to say how, since the last prize giving, 'we have seen something of the strength and weakness of our Empire. We might well be proud of the British Empire, although it has its faults.' He rounded off his speech by reproving 'those men in England who were shirking their responsibilities and having their twopence-halfpenny strikes about nothing, while others are giving their lives.'

Those assembled in the school hall were reminded how the King, when he was the Prince of Wales, had said after his tour of the British Empire, 'England must wake up'. The Revd Bingham said they should all be more self-sacrificing and patriotic, and hoped that, by the end of the war, the nation would be more united than ever before in its glorious history – and the outcome to be a great victory for the British Empire.

The pianist then struck up with 'God Bless the Prince of Wales'. By then, Hilda, secure in the knowledge that the prize was truly hers, sang fervently with the others.

> Among our ancient mountains,
> And from our lovely vales,
> Oh! let the prayer re-echo,
> God bless the Prince of Wales!

Nobody seemed to want the morning to end, unlike when they were having an arithmetic lesson.

A boy raised his hand. 'Could we have "Here's a Health Unto His Majesty" before we go please, seeing as we've sung "God Bless the Prince of Wales". We don't want to leave anybody out, do we sir?' The pianist complied vigorously, as the music score advised.

Hilda by that time was feeling a little upset for those who hadn't won, but no one looked in any way dismayed, and all were still joining in with tremendous gusto. 'Here's a health unto His Majesty, With a fal lal lallala la la la . . .' By that time the hands of the big, round clock were almost at noon.

The Vicar called for three cheers for Hilda, the worthy prizewinner, three more, 'for our sailors and soldiers', then prayers for those in peril on land and sea every day while the conflict raged. He then asked all the children to stand for, 'God Bless Our Native Land', sung to the tune of the National Anthem.

> God bless our native land,
> May heaven's protecting hand

Still guard our shore,
May peace her power extend,
Foe be transformed to friend,
And Britain's power depend
On War no more.

Hilda thanked Mr B. Hutton-Croft once more for the lovely book, which, she assured him, she would treasure all her life. (This she did, it still has pride of place in my bookcase.)

The schoolchildren dispersed for their 'well earned half-day holiday', as the Vicar put it, the flags and bunting were put away for another year, and Hilda, feeling as though she had wings on her feet and joy in her heart, ran off through the little lane, home to Jasmine Cottage, to proudly show off her Empire Day prize.

## CHAPTER 21

# A New Beginning

With such songs and words as their background, it is no wonder that the generation of youth from the Great War years were of such noble spirit and self-sacrificing ways. Their schooling bred within them a strong moral backbone, the rousing tunes and inspiring words imbuing them with a generosity and kindliness of spirit that made courage come naturally to them.

Indeed, even before being called upon to fight on land and sea – though many volunteered – they had to have courage in more localized situations. The day, for instance, when the schoolmaster announced that the dentist had arrived in the district. One of the local shops letting him a room.

When many families could not afford to buy commercial toothpastes they thought that rubbing teeth with soot kept them from discolouration, strange as it may seem. Others wet a piece of linen and dipped it in cigar dust before rubbing their teeth vigorously with it. (Though few smoked cigars, except on Christmas Day.)

Any child whose teeth needed the attention of the dentist, though he or she may feel pain and no anaesthetic numbed the process of extractions, had utmost faith in the professional man. Although sometimes the brass band played in the square to deaden the squeals.

The dentist charged a shilling or so for his services. When one of the Haigh children required attention they had to go by themselves, their mother unable to stand the mental torture of being there watching – and maybe hearing – the commotion, if any. Instead, she had a drop of brandy then stood in the doorway of Jasmine Cottage to await their return. A tragic-looking figure, on tenterhooks until Hilda, Ella, Winnie, or whoever had toothache reappeared, swollen-jawed but triumphant.

'Did he get the tooth out all right?' she quavered, her pent-up emotions overflowing in tears. The patient was then ushered into the 'boudoir', made more welcoming with a crackling fire in winter. When Hilda had a tooth out she stayed away from school the rest of the day, a thick knitted scarf tied round her jaw to keep out draughts. Her way of coping with pain was to think herself out in the mud-filled trenches of France, cold, hungry, and facing the Germans. If her brothers Ernie and Willie could endure all that, surely she could face having a tooth out! The thing was to think of something else, Hilda always said, and remember the advice in those Empire Day songs. Be brave, have faith in God – and the dentist.

*Hilda aged fourteen and about to become the milliner's apprentice.*

Ghastly tales were recounted in the schoolyard next day; this almost made the experience worthwhile, for the pleasure of recounting it and being the Hero of the Hour. The pain, the gore – and if one had a tooth to display, wonderful! But the hole where the tooth had been wrenched from its roots still felt fragile if there was a drill lesson, and toes had to be touched without bending the knees. There were no swimming lessons, so someone who had had a tooth out need not be excused from attending, but some of the boys learned to swim in the river – how daring.

When Hilda was in the top standard at school, she and another girl were entrusted with washing the plants which were arrayed on the classroom window-sills. These were mainly aspidistras. This was done on Friday afternoons when the younger children were engaged in 'private reading'.

How carefully Hilda nurtured those plants, tip-toeing back into the quiet classrooms and replacing them, glossy and shining after their bath. She imagined the dark green leaves seemed to thank her as they took their places on the dark brown window-sills. Their positions were always varied, so they would have a different view and not get bored. Sensitive to the feelings of others, Hilda's concern readily extended to all living creatures, even to the plants and flowers.

It was the summer of 1915, Hilda was fourteen, and it was time to be thinking about what type of work she would like to take up on leaving her beloved school. Although the teachers agreed wholeheartedly that, until she did decide what to do, she was more than welcome to go and help with the infants' class, if ever she felt like it.

Before joining the West Yorkshire Regiment, Ernie had been learning to be a cobbler. Alec and George had no hesitation as to what careers they wanted – to follow in their father's footsteps and be policemen. The former was in the Dewsbury police force, George at Harrogate. When the war began Willie became a soldier, later a policeman too.

While finances were improving in the Haigh family, and there was more room in the cottage as some moved away, Big Changes were afoot. Familiar faces were missing, as young men volunteered for the Army and the Navy, then the news began to filter back of those who had been wounded, some fatally. The happy, carefree years were over.

However, the villagers were thankful for the blessings they had, always attending church on Sundays to give thanks and say prayers for those less fortunate. There were plenty of vegetables in the big garden at the back of Hilda's house, and apples galore from the trees in the orchard. One bright morning, when Hilda called in at Miss West's, the milliner, to select some hats 'on appro' for her mother, the lady in the floor-length black dress said to the pretty, polite fourteen-year-old, 'I hear you have left school now.'

'Yes, Miss West.' The milliner, flanked with beautiful hats in all shapes and hues, smiled at the young girl, neatly dressed in a long, dark serge skirt and long-sleeved white blouse, with a dark hat pulled rakishly to one side.

'I've been looking out for a suitable girl to help in the shop, to dress the windows and trim the hats and children's bonnets attractively. Do you think that you would care for the work, my dear?'

Hilda's immediate, instinctive response was to fling her arms round that genteel lady's neck and kiss her. There was nothing she would like better! Not for her the ordeal of 'adding up' in a shop or similar means of earning a living, anything artistic was much more in her line! She flashed a smile of pure delight and promised to ask her Mama, and thanked Miss West so much for her very kind offer, and for doing Hilda the honour of asking her.

*A humorous postcard depicting a lady's familiar dilemma when visiting a hat shop with her husband.*

# CHAPTER 22

# The Milliner's Apprentice

Before the onset of the Great War, no self-respecting girl would be seen outside without a hat. Hilda was captivated by the millinery creations she saw her mother and other ladies of the village wear, and the myriad of styles pictured in the periodicals that she read: *The Girl's Own Paper*, *Woman's Magazine* and *Forget-Me-Not*.

How elegant were the girls' hats for spring, even though they were only illustrated in black and white, they were visions of loveliness. A tam-o'-shanter crown, trimmed with pink roses, or a dressy hat trimmed with large poppies and a ruching of lace, a felt hat underlined with straw, and trimmed with a fancy scarf. For afternoon wear, how about a 'Black Chip' hat trimmed with large roses and foliage? Or, a large boater, silk pleating showing above and below the velvet band. The tendency of new hats designed in the last year before hostilities began was for them to be shaped long rather than wide. Some of the larger shapes drooped gracefully at front and back, smaller hats for the most part turned right up off the face. Ostrich tips and feathery effects were fashionable for decoration.

Middle-aged women favoured rather small hats or toques. Flowers, in combination with lace, feathers, velvet and other materials were popular as trimmings. Lace was used in various ways. One toque had a heavy lace band to match that used on the lapels of a coat. In another design, lace was used with velvet. 'A velvet-lined brim suited most faces', readers were assured.

In the magazine *Forget-Me-Not*, despite the Suffragette movement and calls for equal pay with men, most young ladies were happy enough to be 'ladylike' in their dress and behaviour. Even if a girl didn't earn much, most could 'run up' a skirt or dress at home from remnants, and magazines were beginning to increase readership by giving away gifts. *Forget-Me-Not* priced one penny, out on Wednesdays, had a beguiling illustration of a demure young lady, wearing an enormous hat and a long, fringed shawl, draped over a floor-length dress, with her hands hidden in an enormous muff. She appeared on the November issue in 1913.

Hilda kept her magazines to read over and over again. Above the cover illustration were the words, 'Hats and Evenings Dresses Given Away'. Well, what fashion conscious young lady could resist that? Imagine, an advert, 'An Evening Frock for Twopence!' The Editress wrote: 'If you would like one of the absolutely charming gowns I have designed especially for my girls, buy another copy of this number. Write the name and address of the friend to whom you present the copy

HATS & EVENING DRESSES GIVEN AWAY.

# FORGET-ME-NOT

No. 1149.]    *Photo: Foulsham & Banfield.*    PRICE ONE PENNY.  OUT ON WEDNESDAY.    [November 15th, 1913.

*The cover picture of the* Forget-Me-Not *magazine, dated 15 November 1913. These cheerful publications helped lift the gloom and sadness generated by the Great War.*

across one coupon, fill up the coupon of your own copy on the ruled lines, as directed, and send the two, pinned together, before November 22nd. Why do you think YOU should have a frock?' A space followed for the reason, and for the name and address. 'Envelopes, "Frocks" to Editress of *Forget-Me-Not*, Gough House, Gough Square, London EC. Thus, by the expenditure of twopence – one penny postage and an extra copy of F.M.N. – you have the chance of obtaining an exquisite little evening gown.'

Of course, Mrs Haigh would never countenance her daughters going to a ball, or even a village dance, so there wasn't much point in wasting twopence.

How exciting when the weekly magazine came out! There were frequent knitting, crochet and fancywork prizes if a girl excelled in any of those directions. Two 10*s* prizes, eight half-crowns, twelve camisoles every week, and a £5 note once a month for a 'Clever Knitter'. Hilda wasn't, she preferred making hats out of odds and ends, but she enjoyed the 'Confidential Chat' page which also gave names of the six hat winners. To enter this, one must fill in the coupon in the magazine describing 'the hat of your dreams', the hat you have long wanted, but, perhaps, have not been extravagant enough to give yourself. This was followed by the tantalizing, 'Wouldn't you like a hat for *nothing*?' The senders of the six short descriptions the Editress considered the best, were given a hat each, made by one of the great millinery houses, Messrs Henry Glave & Co., New Oxford Street, London W.

The coupon in the magazine remains unfilled. Two winners were Miss Maude Evans, then of 36 Herne Hill Road, Loughboro' Junction, S. E., and Miss Grace Fletcher, Royal Hotel, Plymouth. Maybe Hilda thought there was little chance of winning in a nationwide magazine.

Hilda was also fascinated by the queries sent in by other readers, and the replies that came from the Editress.

'"I.G.T." – No books will teach you half as much about everyday ways and customs as the habit of noticing what other people do, especially those in the society you wish to frequent. Be very quiet and modest, and not above taking a hint, when kindly meant, and you will not make any very serious mistakes. I am so glad that your husband is making such rapid progress in his profession. I am sure that he is proud of you also. You are quite right to keep step with him as he rises socially.'

Other people's lives – how could any girl ever feel bored, when such a diversity of problems and ways of life were to be read about? Reading, thought Hilda, was still the best leisure interest of all, even though she had outgrown fairy tales. Other girls' problems, however, only served to reaffirm Hilda's belief in how fortunate she was in being a country constable's daughter, and one who would shortly be a milliner's apprentice. What a happy life she had! Reading on, how relieved she was not to be like 'Marjorie', who was in love with a first cousin. The reply from the Editress was, 'it is absolutely legal to marry your first cousin, and only advisable not to when there is an unhappy family history of insanity or some such hereditary disease.'

Yes indeed, how very lucky were the Haigh family. They were all fit and well, both mentally and physically. But when 'everything in the garden is lovely' as the saying goes, how long can it last? Ah well, begone dull care, there was a war on, and Alec, George, Willie and Ernie were by then part of it. Hilda read on.

November 15, 1913.    FORGET-ME-NOT SUPPLEMENT.    157

## Do YOU Want a Hat for Nothing? *(See Coupon on page 149.)*

Miss Winnie Burrows, 8, Berlior Road, Catford, writes : "My beautiful hat has just arrived. Oh, I am so full of happiness that I don't quite know where I am, and I really don't know how to thank you enough for it. I can only say I thank you with all my heart, which I really do. If only you could see me in it ! It's just the last word in smartness."

Miss Minnie E. Donough, Wrottesley Road, Tettenhall, Wolverhampton, wrote : " The hat I should love is a dull, stone-blue velour, slightly boat-shaped, with an upturned brim, and trimmed with a smart feather mount."

Miss E. J. Smith, Romsdal, Florence Road, Sanderstead, wrote: "My ideal hat arrived quite safely this morning. I cannot tell you how delighted I am with it; it suits me perfectly. I am sending the postcards to my friends, only hoping they will become readers of the delightful F.-M.-N."

Mrs. Cowman, Glenside, Beansty, Whitehaven, wished for " a simple French sailor shape, covered with black satin, with a fold of turquoise-blue velvet draped round the crown, and finished with a long white brush osprey at the left side."

Mrs. G. Ainley, Collinson's Cafe, Port Erin, I.O.M., desired " a good-sized turban-shaped seal hat, with upturned brim, finished with an Oriental beaded ornament at the left side"

Miss G. Chisnall, Woodville, The Grove, Isleworth, wrote : " I cannot tell you how surprised I was to find that I had been a winner in your competition, as I had given up hope long ago of getting my ideal hat. I was perfectly charmed with the model, which quite comes up to my best hopes of my ideal, and do wish to thank you most sincerely for it."

Miss Jean McGregor, 81, Queen Street, Galashields, Scotland, asked for " a soft, dark brown velour in a long shape, turned up a little all round, and trimmed with a narrow band of Oriental silk, and a small feather mount at the side."

Miss Kitty Spencer, N. Newbald, Brough, E. Yorks, wanted " a large, black beaver hat, turned up all round, but wider at the sides, and caught up at the front with a golden plume, and a cord the same shade round the crown."

**These delightful hats were made by Messrs. Henry Glave & Co., of New Oxford Street, London, W.**

*'Do you want a hat for nothing?' These were magic words to Hilda, especially when she was working in the milliner's shop. Again, this extract is from* Forget-Me-Not.

At the end of the page was an invitation: 'Do join my Club if you are a nice girl and I'm sure you are ARE!' Hilda wondered if all the others were. How about 'Maykins'? Her reply from the Editress was, 'Your lover's jealousy is quite natural. Try very hard to make him realise that you love no one but himself, and avoid your former sweetheart whenever it is possible.' Well, when Hilda was employed in the little bow-windowed millinery shop down the road, there would be little chance of *her* getting entangled with any young men there.

Hats, glorious hats, hats of all shapes and sizes, she turned again to regard the illustrations of the hats the six readers had won. Miss Minnie E. Donough of Wolverhampton had written, 'The hat I should love is a dull, stone-blue velour, slightly boat-shaped, with an upturned brim, trimmed with a smart feather mount.'

Mrs Cowhan of Whitehaven wished for, 'a simple French sailor shape, covered with black satin, with a fold of turquoise blue velvet draped round the crown, and finished with a long, white brush of osprey at the left side.' A large, black, beaver hat, turned up all round but wide at the sides and caught up at the front with a golden plume, with a cord the same shade around the crown was the choice of Miss Kitty Spencer, of Brough, East Yorkshire.

A 'Scottish lass', Miss Jean McGregor, had asked for, 'a soft, dark-brown velour in a long shape, turned up a little all round and trimmed with a narrow band of oriental silk, with a small feather mounted at the side.'

Mrs G. Ainley from Collinson's Café, Port Erin, Isle of Man, desired a good sized, turban-shaped seal hat, with the upturned brim finished with an Oriental beaded ornament on the left side. The hat won by Miss E.J. Smith of Florence Road, Sanderstead, was not illustrated, but she wrote, 'My ideal hat arrived quite safely this morning. I cannot tell you how delighted I am with it, it suits me perfectly. I am sending the postcards to my friends, only hoping that they will become readers of the delightful *Forget-Me-Not*.'

Miss Annie Herbert pictured her hat as, 'a pretty, soft grey beaver, very small and close fitting, with a turned-up brim, and trimmed with a band of purple velvet laid round the crown, finished with a flat bow and a bunch of Parma violets at the left side.'

There was no chance of idle hands getting into mischief when reading those magazines for girls. There was such a lot to make, such a lot of help to give to others with the outlay of a bit of time and any odds and ends. If readers became members of the *Forget-Me-Not* club they could exchange all manner of things. A girl from Chesham wanted orders for knitted stockings, knee caps, hot-water bags, night socks, also aprons and tea-cloths. Her work was beautifully done and her charges reasonable.

A member from Salisbury excelled in beautiful, hand-knitted lace, and would be pleased to receive orders. Member No. 45071, Plymouth, 'embroiders handkerchiefs very nicely. Her charges vary from 1*d* to 4*d* for embroidery only. The handkerchiefs are of course extra, and can be supplied by the member if desired.'

Club members had to include their club number on letters when writing to other members via the Editress. An enamelled club badge could be obtained by sending a postal order for sixpence. A gold watch was presented to every thousandth member of the club, a pair of silver and enamel hatpins to every fiftieth member, and a gold brooch given every week to a member selected by the Editress. Girls could also buy club colours, 1s 6d for the tie and band, the tie alone was 1s and the band, 9d.

Every week, the girl who sent the most new members persuaded to 'join our happy band', and enclosed a penny stamp to pay the postage of the membership cards, was sent a beautiful silk and lace blouse, or other gift. A Halifax member wrote, 'I really cannot tell you how delighted I am with it. I have never won anything in my life before, so you can imagine what a surprise it was for me. I am so overjoyed that I must go and have my photo taken in it.' Another week the sender of the second longest list of new members was awarded a pretty, velvet neck-bow with buckle as an extra prize.

A mother can't produce many such geniuses, but Hilda's mother was thrilled enough to learn that her 'Hiltie' had been asked to work for Miss West, and that she wouldn't be leaving home and going into service. With the boys gone to be soldiers, and Hannah away working as a cook, out of her large brood of children she only had Hilda, Ella and Winnie left at home.

She made a point of 'putting on her best bib and tucker' and strolling sedately down to see Miss West, to thank her for selecting Hilda as her apprentice. Secretly, apart from her relief that 'Hiltie' would still be living at home, she did wonder if there might perhaps be the occasional straw or velour hat at a 'knock-down price'. So, Hilda was engaged to work for the milliner at a few shillings a week. There were no travel fares to worry about, and it was only a couple of minutes brisk walk from Jasmine Cottage.

Regret at leaving school was tempered by the idea of this New Adventure; working for Miss West, actually being paid for doing what she loved, and being able to help her dear mama. How importantly, if a little self-consciously, Hilda left Jasmine Cottage on that first morning. A schoolgirl no longer, she wore her ankle-length skirt, blouse demurely caught at the neckline with a small brooch, black stockings and lace-up shoes, her hat was at a rakish angle, with a black ribbon band and hat pins, and her long black hair was caught in a huge bow on the nape of her neck. She even had a wrist-watch and felt so grown up. As ever, she had the usual expression of half-expected surprise on her face, which readily became a full-blown radiant smile. Local boy Clem Mustill – his people had a mineral water works and apartments in St James' Square – happened to see Hilda that first morning as she walked down New Row, and was struck by the lovely smile that she gave him. Her Mama's last words as she waved her daughter goodbye were, 'remember to use your hatpins if you are attacked'. Not much chance of that in such a quiet, God-fearing community as Boroughbridge then was!

Pit-a-pat bumped Hilda's heart as she lifted the sneck of the millinery shop, but Miss West greeted her kindly, and hoped that Hilda would be very happy working there. The rustle of the milliner's long black dress as she moved serenely about the place was a memory that lived long in the heart of her young apprentice.

Mrs. MUSTILL

Sᴛ. JAMES' SQUARE,

ᎯBOROUGHBRIDGE

APARTMENTS:

4 Bedrooms, 2 Sitting-Rooms.

PLEASANTLY SITUATED.

*The Mustill family also had other business concerns, namely the letting of apartments in St James' Square, Boroughbridge.*

In that quaint little establishment Hilda was captivated by the hats, displayed on tall stands on the counters. Bonnets for children were in the tiny window, while the main one was reserved for ladies' millinery. Immediately she knew that she had found her niche in her working life, some girls she knew went from one job to another.

On Mondays, when most of the villagers were busy with wash tubs and mangles, Miss West and her apprentice were busy attending to the appearance of the place. Windows had to be cleaned with chamois leathers, hat stands dusted, displays changed. On 'nippy' mornings a fire had to be lit in the blackleaded grate. An old pair of gloves, kept for that purpose, was used for such work, as no marks must soil the materials.

When all the mundane tasks were completed the pair perched on hard, high wooden chairs either side of the fireplace, the flames soon glowing with a comforting brightness on cold days. Initially, Hilda only watched as her employer decided which artificial flowers and ribbons to decorate hats with. There were two huge deep drawers beneath the counter, full of forget-me-nots, artificial cabbage roses, swathes of beautiful material, bunches of 'cherries' – to the novice milliner, an Aladdin's cave, full of treasure beyond compare.

'Now Hilda my dear, let me see how you'd trim this little beauty.' Miss West handed a child's bonnet to her apprentice who was so eager to learn. She chose tiny, pink, artificial rosebuds and pale green satin rosettes, which she soon learned how to make. Pale pink ribbons to tie beneath a small chin – if she was in Heaven, she couldn't have been happier.

When fond Mamas bustled into 'The Emporium', as they laughingly called the small place, to purchase pretty bonnets or panama hats for their small daughters, Hilda was in her element helping them decide on the most suitable and flattering choice.

She thought they all looked beautiful. Some had waist-length straight, shiny hair, like the drawings of Alice in Wonderland in her prize book. Others had long ringlets. Hilda couldn't resist poking a finger into the silken curls as she adjusted ribbons and bows. One of the bedtime rituals of all small girls was to give their hair a hundred strokes with the brush each night. Those were the days of 'a woman's crowning glory'. If a girl was not conventionally pretty, a mane of clean, shining, healthy hair gave the appearance of beauty – or at least femininity. And, of course, girls were taught that it was the beauty that 'shone from within' that really counted in life. A kind, helpful personality was worth a million 'empty showcases'. Nevertheless, a young lady should make the best of herself, and beautiful hair and a delightful hat did much to achieve that aim.

Tucked out of the sight of customers, in a curtained-off corner, was a gas ring. Every morning, as the church clock struck eleven, Miss West 'downed tools' and cooed, 'Well, are we ready for a little refreshment, Hilda?' The little black iron kettle was filled and soon the friends – for that is what they soon became – were enjoying a mug of cocoa each, with home-made oatcakes from Jasmine Cottage, liberally spread with butter. 'To keep the band in the nick', Mama smiled impishly.

Milliner and apprentice took it in turns to have their midday dinner. Miss West walked to the home of a friend who lived nearby. While she was absent Hilda tried to get as much work done as possible in order to.her the sweet words of praise on her return, 'My word, Hilda, you *have* been busy!' admiringly turning round the latest hat or bonnet. And she had made sure there was no overflow of ashes from the fire, wearing her gloves to do so then washing her hands meticulously. The 'Emporium' always looked neat and tidy.

There were large mirrors, with smaller, wooden-backed, hand-held ones for customers to view themselves in, admiring themselves in their latest millinery creation from all angles. Sometimes, when alone in the dinner hour, the young apprentice paused to regard the reflection of an enchanting-looking young lady, with thick, jet-black hair, a flawless, pale complexion and flashing hazel eyes. Devoid, need it be said, of any shop-bought beauty aids whatsoever.

Those were the days when the customer was always right, no matter how trying some may be. Miss West and Hilda worked according to a charming line of Emerson's: 'Life is not so short but that there is always time for courtesy.' Hilda didn't need to be told to hold the door open until a customer was through the door, with a pleasant, welcoming or departing, 'Good Morning' or 'Good Afternoon'.

How peaceful it was, with nothing but the occasional clatter of horse's hooves on the cobbles outside, the song of birds in summertime. Sometimes Miss West and Hilda sang as they stitched, covering and lining hats with delicate swathes of silks, taffetas, satins and crêpe de Chine.

Mauve was Hilda's favourite shade, it reminded her of a morning sky, weddings, and all things lovely. It was so romantic looking. Having to wear mourning clothes would be no tribulation at all if mauve draperies were allowed. A hat of enormous dimensions was entrusted to her to decorate for a distinguished customer who asked for 'misty mauves, and lilacs'. Hilda attached fragile nun's veiling, adding velvety deep-purple, artificial Parma violets here and there. The customer adored it, and told Hilda she couldn't wait for the wedding to wear it. Lace, velvet, ostrich features, even brilliant artificial scarlet poppies endeared themselves to the artistic young milliner.

Though hats were seldom worn with an evening dress, if a lady had to walk, or go by train or tram to a theatre, a light woollen crocheted 'fascinator' was worn. This was a kind of hood, especially designed for evening wear, and costing only two or three shillings. Silk, chiffon, and lace fascinators were more expensive, but a pretty lace scarf or white crêpe de Chine motor scarf served the same purpose of keeping hair tidy. Fascinators were dress accessories within the scope of most people, and dainty little head coverings were fashioned at home from a length of lace, chiffon, or silk.

With the increasing popularity of the motor car, distinctive motoring millinery and veils were worn. The veil, worn over a hat and tied beneath the chin, served the dual purpose of keeping the hat on and the hair tidy. No more worries on a gusty day of hatpins falling out and tresses becoming loosened and falling about the face in disarray.

Earlier, tight-fitting veils were trying to the eyes, and milliners were advised that large patterns and spots should be avoided. The plainer the pattern and finer the net, the better for the eyesight. When taken off, a veil should be pulled out smoothly, then wound round a piece of cardboard, or else rolled up carefully, the ends being kept even.

It used to be practically *de rigueur* for a girl, as soon as she married, to discard youthful-looking hats for the more sober bonnet, a sign that she had 'attained the dignity of matronhood'. Later, the old-fashioned bonnet was worn only by elderly ladies. In any event, dainty lace and silk creations with jet, ribbons, ostrich tips or other trimmings were created by milliners employed to make them as youthful looking as was compatible with the age of their wearer. A woman of taste shunned extreme styles of millinery and dress: 'no woman should, by her attire, make herself appear grotesque'. For wet weather, waterproof silk hoods were available to cover the hat or bonnet, from 10s 6d and upwards in some establishments.

Unlike many girls who only worked in mill, factory, or domestic service to earn a living, the milliner's apprentice's work was her hobby too. Even at home Hilda loved to concoct hats out of bits of material and flowers, and to renovate old ones.

Besides her hats, Miss West sold bunches of bright red 'pretend' clusters of cherry sprays, for customers to liven up a coat lapel or a dark dress. They could also be used to decorate their 'everyday' headgear themselves.

Hilda often presented Miss West with a bouquet of flowers for the shop counter from the garden of Jasmine Cottage, and apples and pears from the orchard. It was a happy time and the days flew by, as they do when one is happy. When Easter of 1916 arrived Miss West gave Hilda a lovely straw hat, and her mother and sisters were also invited to choose one each from a selection. The songs of the time matched those picture hats perfectly, they were so romantic, both in words and haunting melodies, even though the horrors of the Great War ran parallel with their daily lives. But as long as there were girls in picture hats, delightful music to lift the sometimes downcast spirit, and the reassurance of Eternal Life at church on Easter Sunday, then even those who had lost family members, friends or sweethearts in the battle, could always find hope for the future. Only when there are none of these is hope in danger of dying. Beautiful music can send the spirit soaring to happier spheres than dwelling in this mortal coil.

*Ellaline Terris, one of the great beauties of the day and heroine for Hilda and Miss West, the milliner.*

As Hilda possessed all three, she wouldn't have changed her life for anything. For there was no thrill like that of a brand new Easter bonnet and, working among them, she felt that every day was as good as an Easter Day. No discordant din of mill or factory for her and Miss West. As they created lovely hats they chatted about their collections of picture postcards, music-hall celebrities, Ellaline Terris, sisters Phyllis and Zena Dare, Marie Studholme, Miss Ellen Terry and others. All these celebrities wearing glorious, extravagant clothes and hats, providing ideas for the creations that emerged from that little village emporium.

So they sang as they stitched and handled the delicate materials. Words of popular songs were printed on many of the postcards, and they learned them by heart. Hilda loved to sing.

Let the Great Big World keep turning, never mind if I've got you.
For I only know that I want you so, and there's no one else will do.
You have simply set me yearning, and for ever I'll be true,
Let the Great Big World keep on turning round, now I've found someone like you.

A great sense of joie de vivre best described Hilda, amusing Miss West in leisure moments by prancing round the shop, behind the little bow-fronted windows, pretending to be a music-hall singer. The happy atmosphere in the milliner's shop – or, indeed, any shop – does much to encourage customers to keep on calling. And how the children adored it when, as they tried on one pretty bonnet after another, the dark haired young lady sang to them as they surveyed themselves in the mirrors. The air was alive with laughter and good humour.

Put on your Tat-ta, little girlie,
Do, do what I want you to!
Far from the busy hurly-burly,
I've got lots to say to you.
My head's completely twirly-whirly,
My girl I want you to be –
So put on your tat-ta, your pretty little tat-ta,
And come out, a tat-ta with me.

# CHAPTER 23

# War News

If only it had been as easy to combat the war as some adverts would have had people believe. One, in the *War Budget* on June 1916 proclaimed, 'Every seasoned soldier knows the bracing, satisfying effect of Wrigley's Chewing Gum, and every new recruit should follow "Tommy's" advice, and make a special point of having Wrigley's handy. Carry a few bars with you and you will soon forget the hardships of campaign life. Wrigley's keeps the mouth moist, allays thirst, prevents fatigue, and makes a smoke doubly enjoyable. Besides, it's splendid for digestion and teeth, and it keeps the breath sweet. Be sure and carry a packet in your kit! It lasts a long time. ½*d* per bar, 2 ½*d* per sealed packet 5 bars, or 1*s* 6*d* per complete box of 140 bars.'

Sometimes, looking at pictures in war newspapers and magazines, Hilda could hardly bear to think that she was comparatively safe, while others were undergoing such miseries. Even animals played their part – in Flanders a team of dogs was shown, harnessed like horses, pulling a plough, and photographed while under fire.

There were lady street cleaners in Chiswick, 'filling in' while men went to war. Everybody, it appeared, was 'doing their bit'. Even infants, those at Sunninghall School filling a hospital pillowcase with 'comforts' for the lads. Soldiers' wives decorated the Roll of Honour at Hackney with fresh flowers daily, a ceremony in every street. Schoolchildren throughout the land were 'pulling their weight' helping to plant potatoes.

Hilda read the reports, and saw a picture of a 'postwoman in the Northern district, who had created a speed record on her round'. She wondered, ought *she* to be doing something to help the war effort – apart from knitting khaki scarves at the Girls' Friendly Society? Gloves on four needles were too complicated for her, how did one know which round it was, when all the slim needles were alike? Besides working in the millinery shop, she helped weed the garden at home, as usual, and wrote letters to Ernie, Willie, George and Alec. 'Slackers' were a thing of the past, if there had ever been any.

Other kinds of 'Comforts for Campaigners' were shop-bought. Boots the chemist sold Vermin Powder, 'for the Pest of the Trenches', priced at 9*d* per tin. Their water sterilizers were a veritable life-saver, destroying all typhoid, cholera, and other organisms possibly present in contaminated water. Two of the sterilizer tablets were dropped into the service bottle of drinking water, then allowed to stand for half an hour. (By which time the owner may well have been killed by

*Ernest Haigh, who died from his wounds in the Great War. He had just celebrated his twenty-first birthday.*

gunfire.) Boots sterilizers were approved by the War Office and millions were sent to the British troops. A bottle of fifty cost 1*s*. Tired, weary, aching feet found relief with a tin of Boots Foot Comfort, 'while walking or on the march', priced at 3*d* a tin.

The public were reminded there were no chemists' shops in the trenches. How awful, thought Hilda sadly, but at least she could send her brothers some of those 'Comforts for Campaigners'.

'Tinned Heat' was a little round tin pocket stove, or 'Campaigner's Cooker'. Only 3½ inches in diameter and 1¼ inches high, it contained solidified methylated spirits. It was deemed to be perfectly safe, quite practical and absolutely efficient; an ideal arrangement for a soldier's use in the trenches. If anything *could* be pronounced ideal in those circumstances. 'Tinned Heat' cost 10½*d* each.

Useful too was the pocket case of compressed medicines. This was a compact box, 6¼ inches long and 1½ inches wide, ½ inch deep, and easily carried about. In tablet form, sectioned off, were five simple medicines. Aspirin for rheumatism, neuralgia and headaches. Meloids for a sore throat, Quinine and Phosphorous tablets for nerve strengthening and giving tone to the system. Rapid Cold Cure tablets for the speedy cure of influenza and colds, and Cascara tablets – The Gentle Laxative. (A soldier probably thought twice before taking those.) The pocket case of assorted 'cures' was priced at 2*s* 9*d* a case.

If any had the time – or the inclination – to clean muddy boots, the popular 'Nugget' polish was in 1*d*, 2*d*, and 4 ½*d* tins. If there was time – and water – for a wash, Sunlight Soap was the probable choice, it was so widely advertised.

A battalion of Canadian Foresters arrived in England that summer of 1916, and felled some of the Scotch firs in the Royal Park at Windsor. Some of that timber was destined for lining and flooring the trenches in France.

Everybody and everything in creation seemed to be engaged in war work. Pigeons carried important messages, and Hilda began to wish that either the war would reach a speedy end, or that she was doing something more important than pandering to feminine vanities. She still loved millinery, but circumstances had changed radically since that first carefree morning when she set off down New Row, so full of joy and hope for the future.

News always seemed to be bad, and women were increasingly employed in work that men had done before the war. Some made simple lighters out of flints, to be sent to the 'Front' where matches were prohibited in certain circumstances. One had taken over as a 'milk portress', doing the work of several men who had 'joined the colours'. The Croydon milk portress began work at four a.m. and dealt with 500 cans and churns for each round. In the black and white newspaper photograph Hilda noticed that the young woman wore headgear similar to that of a Quaker girl, with a long-sleeved blouse and dark, ankle-length skirt.

Some actresses were brave enough to go behind the firing line 'somewhere in France' to entertain 'the lads'. Miss Lena Ashwell and her Concert Party were among them. Keeping up morale was as important as physical sustenance. Some soldier musicians were taken out of their trenches to make a tour of the lines, and provide recreation for the pleasure of their comrades-in-arms. Sometimes they performed to several 'houses' a day, along with church parades and visits to convalescent camps. Members of the Salvation Army went to France, entertaining 'Kitchener's Chaps' on the banjo, concertina and guitar. The great actress Sarah Bernhardt aroused great enthusiasm with her performances in the war zone.

Horses as well as soldiers had to be fed and needed attention. French Colonial troops were pictured in a June issue of *The War Budget* making hay and stacking it for use of the cavalry. When Hilda saw Mr Bruce the milkman's horse plodding along peaceably with the churns, happily accepting a carrot from customers on his round, she could hardly bear to think about those horses unlucky enough to be in the midst of shell and cannon.

Everyone was urged to collect waste paper, some of it sold to raise funds for the building of a soldiers' home at Bristol. Make do and mend, and innovation, was the order of the day. Well, it always had been in many homes. 'Waste not, want not' being a motto worth following.

Back in England Zeppelins caused havoc. Hilda's Dad was on his beat during the early hours, walking on the bridge, when one of those huge 'birds of war' droned overhead. He flung himself flat against the side of the bridge thinking, 'it's a bit of a to do when a fellow can't go about his lawful business without a blessed Hun in a Zeppelin threatening him overhead'. His sturdy wooden truncheon was no match for one of those.

In the middle of June 1916 came the news of Lord Kitchener's death on active service, drowned when on board HMS *Hampshire*, sunk either by a mine or torpedo to the west of the Orkneys. 'Death,' it was reported, 'met him on active service, as he would have wished.'

In the millinery shop, Hilda and Miss West discussed the progress of the war as they worked, remarking on how the way women were, besides taking on men's work, even beginning to *dress* like men in some jobs! Girls employed by a

# WRIGHT'S COAL TAR SOAP

### DOCTORS ADVISE IT.

### MOTHERS PRIZE IT.

### THE WISE MAN BUYS IT.

*Purifies the skin and prevents infection.*

**FOUR-PENCE a Tablet.**

*An advertisement for Wright's Coal Tar Soap. This product contributed more to the war effort than perhaps was first expected!*

Basingstoke firm of tomato growers were actually photographed hatless – and wearing dungarees! But what a nightmare had overtaken the glorious Edwardian age – now that soldiers, who erstwhile had enjoyed peaceful childhoods and simple pleasures, were being blinded, shell-shocked, maimed and killed.

Hilda, her normal reading very different from the wartime newspapers, was nevertheless fascinated by the news and different types of adverts. Wright's Coal Tar Soap became known as the 'Soldiers' Soap'. One young soldier's mother wrote – so the advert maintained – that her son, on active service somewhere in France, had written: 'Don't send any vermin powder, thanks; I use Wright's Coal Tar Soap. That's as effective and much more pleasant.'

Normality still reigned, as ever, in the fashion industry. Lloyds Fashions advertised patterns for the home dressmaker, price 2d each. The pattern was inside a sealed envelope which gave a sketch of the garment on the front, and a diagram with full instructions for making on the back. Eighteen garments included a bed wrap, child's bodice and drawers, ladies' combinations, camiknickers, boy's tunic suit, useful skirt, morning blouse, child's coat, and a smocked overall. But one couldn't escape the references to the war for long. For instance, the 'Mesh-Guard' for wrist-watches: 'If your other hand is occupied with rifle or clubs or tools, there's no need to drop them. Glance at the dial in the usual way. Simple, strong, easily attached, the Mesh-Guard in Nickel or Khaki, 1s, or hall-marked silver, 2s, make wrist-watches safe.'

Hilda, though she had always loved the outdoors and walking in the countryside, hardly envied the lady street cleaners pictured in Birmingham, finishing off a road after the tarring and sanding process. But at least they all wore hats as they wielded their long brushes. Women were pictured working on their knees at Hadleigh Farm Colony, after being called upon to be substitutes for male workers. Before the war the Salvation Army provided labour for destitute men, then the substitute female labourers took their places, hoeing onion fields and gathering the crop. The milliner's apprentice was relieved to note that, without exception, all the women wore hats. Queen Mary wore a hat with a tall, curled plume as she drove with King George, who wore army uniform, to the memorial service for Lord Kitchener at St Paul's Cathedral towards the end of June.

Also in June Hilda was saddened to read about the sinking of HMS *Shark*, more so as there was a picture of the ship's cat, Lyddite, shown in the arms of one of the crew. Surely it wasn't fair to take a cat to sea, away from its natural habitat? Fields and woods, then a lovely blazing fire to snuggle in front of in the cold weather. The ship's captain had one of his legs shot away, but fought with his last gun until the ship sank, taking the valiant captain – and the cat – down with it. The news of the pet dog of an ASC battalion proved yet again the courage and devotion of animals. At Cape Helles, it saved the lives of two of the battalion's men. Wounded, the dog was taken to the animal hospital at Victoria.

Increasingly, Hilda worried that making hats was of little importance at that time. Especially when a Miss Hilary Dent, the first lady gamekeeper to be employed on Lord Montagu's Hampshire estate, was pictured looking quite at ease with a great long gun. All Hilda was playing around with was long ostrich feathers. Miss Dent, it was recorded, was a crack shot and skilful forester. No such skills had the milliner's apprentice, but yes, she could play the piano, sing and perhaps entertain – but a piano wasn't like a violin, easy to pack. She saw a photograph of Miss Marie Hall, a famous violinist, giving a private concert to a group of wounded and convalescent Anzacs in her room at a London theatre. Now she'd love to do something like that!

On more down-to-earth topics, *The Mother's Magazine*, 3d, enclosed a pattern for ladies' knickers for day or evening wear in the June number. As well as the pattern, readers could enjoy twenty-two articles, stories, plus a, 'powerful new serial' by Silas K. Hocking, also a special fairy story supplement for children. Hilda was tempted to buy it. What a relief to read about fairies instead of death, doom and disaster. Another magazine, *Coming Fashions*, 6d, had a free pattern for a 'charming summer frock' and scores of suggestions for gowns, costumes, hats and lingerie. Plus there were articles on toilet, home furnishing, cookery, table decoration and housekeeping. 3d and 6d were small prices to pay for ridding one's mind of war and misery.

If the war still continued into 1917, when Hilda became sixteen, she was determined to do something for the war effort. Perhaps become a nurse, or join the Red Cross but not, oh no, not a road sweeper. Yet all manner of unlikely occupations were being taken on by women to release men for the Army and Navy. The National Land Committee sent the first party of women agriculturists

*Examples of the paper dress patterns that could be sent for and made up during the Great War. These examples come from* The Lady's World, *9 August 1904.*

to Donnington Heath, Evesham. They were photographed for the newspaper, cutting cabbages and wearing smocks and huge hats to shield the sun from their faces. 'Pale and interesting' was still more fashionable for ladies' complexions than the tanned, outdoor look.

A Northamptonshire soldier's wife was shown helping her father shear sheep during her husband's absence. She wore a large brimmed boater-type hat. A couple of intrepid young women had become window cleaners, each carrying a ladder and bucket over their shoulders, small, neat hats with turned-up brims on their heads. A lady tram conductor was pictured buying a rose on Rose Day and Queen Alexandra passing through cheering crowds in an open landau, wearing a veiled toque trimmed with feathers. Rose Day, with its thirty million emblems of Royal devotion, was dedicated to the cause of wounded British heroes.

Hilda rather fancied herself in nurses' uniform, she loved the flowing white headgear – and what a marvellous way of making the acquaintance of some of those handsome young men – as long as they weren't *frighteningly* badly wounded. The Lord Mayor of London had opened a Convalescent Home for Canadians at Kingswood, a beautiful estate adjoining Sydenham Hill station. The house was converted by the generosity of Massey-Harris Co. Ltd, of Toronto, makers of agricultural implements.

Women were working in factories, at forge and lathe, and the simpler parts of shell making. An American lady journalist touring the Western Front wrote: 'None but women could be seen working on the land anywhere.' She had witnessed a three-year-old child among lots of orphans. Her Belgian father, fleeing with his child in his arms, was killed by a shell. He clutched her tighter as he fell, and held her for nearly two days though he was dead when she was rescued. The journalist saw soldiers, blinded in battle, being taught how to fence, to type, and other occupations.

Undeterred, volunteers were still offering to fight for their country. Leeds City Council granted £2,000 towards the equipment of the Leeds Battalions of the West Yorkshire Volunteers. Hilda's brother Ernie was in the West Yorkshire Regiment, she prayed for his safety every day, also for Willie, George and Alec, and the family sent parcels and letters frequently. Ernie would be twenty-one that October of 1916, and his mother intended to bake a cake and post it in time for his coming of age. She hoped that it would withstand the journey, and not be opened as a tin full of crumbs. Hilda was so upset when her mother, in church on a Sunday, often dabbed her eyes with her best, lace-edged handkerchief when her favourite hymn was played. It seemed to be a regular occurrence in those uncertain days of war.

> God be with you till we meet again,
> By His counsels guide, uphold you,
> With His arms securely fold you,
> God be with you till we meet again;
> Till we meet, till we meet,
> Till we meet, at Jesus' feet,
> Till we meet, till we meet,
> God be with you till we meet again.

Sarah Eleanor could usually manage the first verse, but was frequently too overcome to continue by the second, rallying only for the third. Perhaps, hoped Hilda, there really was some kind of telepathy that could span the miles and let 'the boys' know they were thought of and prayed for constantly. Hilda's Dad was fond of the hymn 'Onward, Christian Soldiers'. The war inspired many poets and musicians, and Miss Kathleen Bruckshaw wrote 'The Munition Workers' Song' specially for them so they wouldn't feel left out. No amount of amusing little ditties did anything for the gallant wounded horses in France, however. Wounded horses were killed and their 'meat' eaten. Horse sausage was a popular meal. Fat from army slaughter houses was made into candles in the trenches.

Toothache, like the war, was also no respector of time or place. One 'Tommy' was pictured being held down while a British Chaplain officiated as a dentist near the trenches. This was far from the comforting embrace of loved ones at home, or the 'Blue Angels', as the ladies in sky-blue overalls were named, who ministered to soldiers in the free buffet at Euston. Open from six a.m. until midnight, it catered for a thousand clients daily. Most of those 'Blue Angels' wore hats, even when indoors.

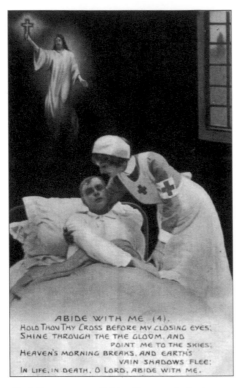

ABIDE WITH ME (4).
HOLD THOU THY CROSS BEFORE MY CLOSING EYES;
SHINE THROUGH THE THE GLOOM, AND
POINT ME TO THE SKIES;
HEAVEN'S MORNING BREAKS, AND EARTH'S
VAIN SHADOWS FLEE;
IN LIFE, IN DEATH, O LORD, ABIDE WITH ME.

*Red Cross nurses did sterling work during the Great War. A Bamforth postcard, posed to evoke such scenes.*

But oh, those poor, helpless animals who couldn't understand what it was all about! Dogs were used by the French as messengers, scouts, sentries and spy hunters. They had special schooling kennels behind the lines, each dog placed under the tuition of one man, who, as his master, taught him the 'arts' of human warfare. One collie, Rover, was pictured wearing a gas mask. Many dogs had shown a fatal curiosity about the German gas.

Hilda could well understand those who volunteered. When the daily newspapers were full of those doing heroic deeds, how could anyone, man or woman, refrain from not doing all they could to help freedom's cause? Indeed, when she saw female members of a northern village fire-brigade riding a motor car and side car, helmets in place instead of hats, she almost felt ashamed of being safe in the shop with dear Miss West.

Day after sickening day, the wounded returned from the Somme, and ladies flung roses in their path as the Red Cross sign on ambulances brought the courageous cargo back to 'Blighty'. Every man, it was said, cheerful and undaunted by his experiences.

Hilda's mother, who usually went into raptures when the vivid red poppies appeared in the garden of Jasmine Cottage, seemed to regard them as an ill omen that summer. 'They look like so much blood', she murmured sadly, as she walked down the garden path to gather the luscious raspberries from the bushes in the back garden.

War made everything different. Even the beautiful poppies which before had been an emblem of beauty, were now, it seemed, one of death and destruction.

# CHAPTER 24

# Stormy Weather

Ordinary life went on. Many a game of cricket was played between wounded servicemen and nurses, the latter wearing hats, the 'umpire' a huge pair of gauntlet gloves. Elsewhere, new wounded comrades were being hauled to safety from the fields of Picardy.

Often, cats were found in the trenches; hunting mice and birds among the wire entanglements of no man's land, walking on trench parapets to have a scrap with the 'next door' tabby. Unperturbed by the whine of bullets, they continued to sit washing their faces with scrupulous care. Should a bullet venture too close, and mud or sand be suddenly showered over them, they retreated into their respective trenches, spitting fiercely.

One day the orangey-coloured Marmaduke cat ventured too far and a German bullet wounded him. Unable to crawl back to his friends in the trench, he lay mewing sadly for help. At nightfall one of the brave soldiers crawled to the stricken cat and brought back the injured casualty. There happened to be a vet among the soldiers, who bound up the wounds, then it was nursed back to health in a miniature dug-out made specially for it. Larks, thrushes and blackbirds were also among the pets kept at the Front. Soldiers found amusement capturing mud turtles in marshes and swamps, and small tortoises were used for 'racing'.

One soldier's pet was a pony named Polly, of the transport section of Mountain Battery. Polly saw service in a number of campaigns, and became fond of her driver. She could detect the whine of a shell, long before the humans heard it. In Gallipoli she used to throw herself flat on the ground at the first sound of one approaching. Other horses and mules cantered about, frantic with fear, but Polly lay down, stretching out her forelegs and, shutting her eyes, played dead. If her driver didn't follow suit however, Polly raised her head, gazed reproachfully at him, and whinnied imploringly, begging him to make haste.

That hot, sultry summer of 1916 must have been more uncomfortable than ever for 'the four-footed Army Service Corps'. For transport of ammunition and medical supplies in exposed situations, a Major Richardson trained some Airedale terriers, which were then officially 'on active service'. One carried blanket and Red Cross equipment strapped round its body, another bearing a load of shells, one with messages in a satchel tied round its back. Such animals, Hilda thought when reading about them, were not even volunteers. They were conscripted, whether they liked it or not. The Kaiser had caused the war. Why should animals have to suffer for the greed of mankind?

*Typical postcards that were sent during the Great War.*

How she hated the Kaiser, and any German who might be wounding her brothers. They hadn't wanted a war either, nor had all the millions of other innocent young men whose ill fortune it had been to be of an age to fight at that time.

That summer, Hilda recalled, days often began in a flood of golden glory then ended in a violent storm. As if, symbolically, the weather was behaving like those glorious Edwardian days of her childhood, before the storm of battle.

Her Mama was absolutely terrified of thunder and lightning, more so if Arthur William was out on duty in the dark, wartime night. Nevertheless, ashen-faced, she tried to 'put on a brave face', for the sake of the children. At the first indication of rough weather, a gathering together of ominous looking, dark grey clouds, she feverishly pulled down the dark green window blinds, turned mirrors to the wall, and pushed cutlery and scissors out of sight in drawers.

Hilda, Ella and Winnie were urged to take cover beneath the kitchen table, draped with the large, plum-coloured chenille cloth. 'Get under, get under, quickly,' her voice commanded, as though to a pack of dogs. Then, with trembling hands, she filled the black iron kettle with water and put it on the hob. The fire was always lit, even in summertime, in order to do the cooking on the blackleaded Yorkshire range. How stifling it was, but safer than being outside, at least the door could be left wide open. Should a thunderbolt decide to enter the Haigh domain, it could then get out through the door, so Mama reasoned. The very thought that it may decide to get beneath the table among them all didn't bear thinking about.

When caught out in a storm, Hilda could never remember whether it was better to take cover beneath a tree from the hail and rain, or stay out in the open. What a waste to be struck with a flash of lightning, much more glorious if it were a German bullet.

But underneath that sturdy table a cup of tea was a Great Sustainer, even against the threat of air attack by Zeppelins or other newfangled horrors that might be lurking and waiting to pounce in the world outside. Enclosed in the darkened cottage, huddled together beneath the table, hardly daring to breathe, Hilda sometimes thought she'd collapse from a combination of heat and fear. Every time the thunder rolled and the lightning flashed, Sarah Eleanor clutched her heaving bosom, moaning 'Oh, my God' and they all had to say the Lord's Prayer.

Hilda frantically cast her mind back over the past few days to recall what, if any, trespasses she had committed. It would have been a bigger catastrophe than ever if their Mama, who had to cut holes in her shoes for her bunions to protrude, had poured boiling water over them in the dim light. Wearing shoes a size too large didn't make for safe walking at the best of times. Sometimes Hilda and Ella had a fit of the giggles. When God was prayed to watch over them, did that mean he had to take care of bunions too? Goading each other on to hysterics they wondered if there'd be any bunions on the battlefield.

When all the precautions she could think of had been taken, their Mama then sat down in the far corner of the room.

'Never face a fireplace in a storm, if a thunderbolt hurtles down the chimney you never know *what* can happen,' the voice droned on. She was, to her children, an Authority on Storms.

When everything was as lightning-proof as it possibly could be, in the interval between one flash and the next, their mother reached to the high mantelpiece for the biscuit barrel. A shaking hand pushed three or four big home-made Shrewsbury biscuits beneath the plush cloth.

'Now don't choke,' they were warned, '*I* won't be able to save you if you do.' This took some of the solace out of their munching. Life seemed beset with problems those days. Which would be worse, to choke to death on one of Mama's Shrewsbury biscuits, be smitten in two by a stroke of lightning, or be bombed by a Zeppelin?

Waiting for the storm to pass gave Hilda an idea of what eternity may be like. Maybe something like those moments beneath the kitchen table, moments that were felt to go on forever, when real life was suspended, a bit like the grandfather clock when it stopped, and the pendulum hung limp, waiting for its Creator to thump life back into it. The feeling that to take another breath would precipitate Something Awful, so you tried not to. A thousand years pass in the twinkling of an eye – so it is said in the Bible – but not so during those summer storms.

When the faint glimmer of sunlight and calm flickered through the blind as it was cautiously lifted, all of them heaved a communal sigh of relief. They emerged, gasping for air, while their Mama assumed – now that danger was past – a nonchalant air. 'Now that little spot of bother is over and done with I think we'll have a bit of a sing-song, shall we?'

Off they trooped into the tiny 'boudoir' which was dominated by the harmonium. Arthur William called his wife 'Sarah Bernhardt' at times of drama as her moods swung so dramatically from tragedy to gaiety. The sing-song usually began with, 'Pack Up your Troubles in your Old Kitbag', tears and smiles fighting for supremacy on her face. This was her kind of mystic thanksgiving for their safe deliverance from the Awful Storm. She even found time to play ludo with them for ten minutes, so heartfelt was her relief that they had all emerged 'in one piece'.

It was almost worth enduring a storm for those few precious moments snatched from the endless round of baking, washing, ironing, blackleading, pegging a rug, and scores of other domestic chores.

If a storm blew up during the night and Dad was out on duty when they were all safe in bed, Hilda could not sleep. There was the never-to-be-forgotten night when the Zeppelin passed over Boroughbridge. It made such a din in the still of the night that the children were urged to get out of their beds. Shivering more from fright than cold, they had the usual tea and big Shrewsbury biscuits underneath the table. That time their Mama crouched there with them, in her voluminous flannelette nightgown, boudoir cap and all, praying in an incoherent, mumbling kind of way, forgetting where she'd got to in the Lord's Prayer, and having to go back to the beginning again. A bit like when, in a lazy fashion, you say your prayers in bed, and are nearly asleep before they are said. 'Our Father, Who art in Heaven,' then a sob, and the Lord was kept waiting again.

When the constable wearily returned from duty he related how he had been walking on the bridge when the Zeppelin had rumbled overhead and he'd flung himself down, praying not so much for his own safety but for those at home in Jasmine Cottage.

'All's well that ends well,' he remarked, reaching for his favourite pipe before 'sleeping it off'.

Hilda didn't recall any food shortages during the 1914–18 war, probably because of the large garden and orchard at the back of the cottage. Their Mama also had the ability to concoct a sustaining, warming stew out of a variety of vegetables. Hannah, her eldest daughter, took after her in that way. When Hannah worked as a cook at Kirby Hall, the coalman who called there remarked he'd never had a better cup of cocoa anywhere than the ones Hannah Haigh made him.

It was a pity there wasn't a banana tree and orange grove too. But the cellar shelves were packed with apples and Sarah Eleanor put a handwritten note on the garden gate, '3d a bagfull of apples'. Then the children gathered blackberries in autumn, so the family didn't feel at all deprived. Arthur William was in the rifle club, but Hilda didn't remember if it was merely as a hobby or whether the men 'shot anything for the table'.

Hilda loved working in the garden, rejoicing when a huge vegetable marrow pushed its 'nose' up through the rich brown earth; pure magic. If it wasn't for the awful war, life would be so wonderful. The gorgeous aroma of redcurrant, raspberry, blackcurrant and gooseberry jams being stirred in the massive preserving pan, how much better than buying it ready-made in jars from the grocer's. Sarah Eleanor hoped that her boys might come on leave before long and be able to take a few jars of home-made jam back with them.

*The bridge over the River Ure in Boroughbridge. It is here that PC Haigh had his close encounter with a low-flying Zeppelin.*

One bright, golden morning in October a letter arrived from Ernie. 'Thank you for the 21st birthday cake,' he had written, 'I shared it with the lads, we ate it in the trench. How it reminded us of dear old Blighty, good old Boroughbridge and all of you at home.' He sent his love, and hoped to be with them before long.

So the big fruit cake hadn't ended up as a load of crumbs after all. 'What an enormous relief!' sighed his mother, when she received the good news. Ernie had managed to reach his twenty-first birthday and was safe. What a party and homecoming they would have when it was over and they could all meet again.

A few days later there was further news of Ernie written by a nurse in hospital, where, she was so sad to report, he lay dying of gunshot wounds. Then the dreaded telegram came informing them that Private Ernest Roland Haigh had 'died for King and Country' on the 16 October 1916.

Everything seemed to stand still. Nothing, not even the little tot of brandy that Ernie used to fetch for his mother could do her any good at that moment. The only small crumb of comfort was that his birthday cake had reached him intact. When his body was brought home she asked if she could have a last glimpse of her son. But his father thought it best that she keep her pleasant memories of their beloved Ernie intact. The happy-go-lucky lad had had his leg shot off, and suffered various other mutilations too.

A military funeral was arranged, and the soldiers of his West Yorkshire Regiment gathered in the churchyard to sound the last post. It was an Indian summer, a hot, sultry, golden afternoon when the once handsome Ernie was laid to rest. The air hung heavy and oppressive over the group of mourners standing, heads bowed, round the graveside. The silence was broken only by the cry of a bird, and the stifled sobs of his mother and sisters.

*A poignant family group. Hilda's parents' gravestone and Ernest Haigh's gravestone; their last resting place in Boroughbridge.*

Six khaki-clad figures had carried the coffin to the grey stone church. Hilda stood, disbelieving, in a black coat, veiled hat, and black gloves, stockings and shoes, thinking that never again would she be able to bear to knit khaki 'comfort' scarves in the quiet evenings when they worked by the light of the oil lamp at the Girls' Friendly Society, knowing that Ernie would never wear khaki again, or any other colour. She would be reminded too much of that small wooden cross up at the top corner of the churchyard which marked the mortal remains of her brother. But time marches on, and the shop in the village that had set aside a room for the 'Collection of Comforts for the Boys' didn't have to wait too long before Hilda saw it as her duty to 'pick up the threads of life again'.

But that day, as the mourners walked slowly, reluctantly, back up the little front garden path the stillness was suddenly disturbed by a low, rumbling sound. Another Zeppelin? They hurried into the cottage and Sarah Eleanor pulled down the blind as a flash of lightning zig-zagged across the darkening sky. Yet she seemed strangely unafraid, as she stood there, too deep in her sorrow to even bother covering up the mirror.

'Thank God,' she breathed, face upturned to the vast, black clouds hanging in the skies as she stood at the doorway, gazing towards the church and the way they had come.

'Thank God, it's only a storm.'

# CHAPTER 25

# Hilda, a Wartime Post Girl

After the initial period of grief and mourning, Hilda's father tried to encourage his family to regard Ernie's passing as a blessing. Not for him years of pain, maybe blindness, and then, to be forgotten when the war was over. No, the name of Ernest R. Haigh would be immortalized forever when the war memorial was erected, along with Ernest R. Bedell, Tom Needham, Charles F. Bryan, Charles Burborough, Guy A. Burnsides, Raymond F. Calvert, John R. Dean, Arthur W. Ellis, Tom Ellis, Arthur Ellison, Arthur Hall, George E. Hall, Arthur Horner, Fred Lancaster and others. Ernie's name was eventually on a plaque in the church too. Indeed, the Haighs were fortunate, only one son gone, while some families had lost two, sometimes more. And that one son, Ernie, had lived an honest, decent life. How much worse a fate to have had a son who brought sorrow to the world, far better a brief, good life than one long one that made others unhappy.

'One day, hinny, one day we will meet again,' the constable consoled his wife. In the meantime, he broke into his favourite, 'Onward, Christian Soldiers, Marching as to war, With the cross of Jesus, Going on before.' The others joined in, 'Christ, the Royal Master, Leads against the foe, Forward into battle, see his banners go!'

Eventually Sarah Eleanor accepted what could not be changed, and was thankful that her son's trials were over. As the November Armistice words are repeated year after year:

> Age shall not weary them
> Nor the years condemn,
> At the going down of the sun
> And in the morning,
> We will remember them.

There was still Willie, then a corporal in the West Yorkshire Regiment, George, Alec, 'Hiltie', Ella and Winnie. The eldest daughter, Hannah, was in great demand as a high-class cook. Somehow or other her parents had managed to send her to both France and Italy for tip-top training.

*The war memorial. Ernest Haigh's name is round the other side.*

Arthur William had a sister in Huddersfield who had 'married well', perhaps she had helped finance Hannah's training. Hilda didn't know how it came about. Certainly no expense had needed to be outlaid for *her* training as a milliner – dear Miss West had taught her all she needed to know. Besides, she didn't think she'd have dared venture to those 'foreign fields', especially on her own.

But Hannah's career flourished. She was in demand at stately homes, and for a time worked for the Princess Marie Louise at Bamborough Castle when exclusive dinner parties were held. Before she attained such status, when she was a young girl employed somewhere for the first time, Hannah once wrote home complaining about someone in authority. Her father had replied immediately, writing in red ink: 'Learn to be commanded before you can command.' And that was that.

Yes, all the children were to be proud of and now, at least, Ernie was at peace, and safe in the old churchyard, far nearer than when he had been in an unknown place under German fire. Sarah thought she mustn't be self-pitying, she had a lot to be thankful for and in the course of time, she and Arthur William would join him.

About that time the post office was in need of a girl to deliver the mail, another young man having enlisted. Much as Hilda adored her work, and couldn't think of anyone she'd rather work for than Miss West, she remembered her Empire Day essay, and all the talk about sacrifice and patriotism. She, Hilda Haigh, daughter of the village policeman and sister of a valiant soldier who fell in battle, wasn't just somebody who *talked* and wrote about those aspirations, was she? No, actions spoke louder than words as her Dad was forever telling his offspring.

Hilda's mind was made up. Her conscience wouldn't allow her to continue living an idyllic life when others were facing such ghastly situations. She took up the second verse of 'Onward, Christian Soldiers', the light of battle shining in her eyes:

> At the name of Jesus
> Satan's host doth flee,
> On then, Christian soldiers,
> On to victory;
> Hell's foundations quiver,
> At the shout of praise,
> Brothers, lift your voices,
> Loud your anthems raise –
> Onward, Christian soldiers, marching as to war . . .

She invited Ella and Winnie to march round the garden with her, waving branches, pretending they were swords, and defying the 'Hun' to beat the Haighs or any other English home. Her parents fully understood her feelings, not to live a life of ease and pleasure while her brothers and so many of their friends and neighbours were facing the enemy. Still too young to train as a nurse, at least she'd feel she was on 'active service', releasing someone to go and fight.

*Willie Haigh in uniform.*

Miss West, however, was dismayed when her young apprentice announced her intention to become a post girl, but realized that was part of the reason why she liked and admired Hilda so much, her consideration for others. Hilda would still bring her apples from their orchard, and when the war was over, she could always go back.

Mr Topham, at the post office, taught her how to sort and deliver the mail. In the dark evenings and mornings of winter, letters had to be sorted by candlelight. But how important it was that communications reached their destination when expected, and that those anxiously awaiting news from a son, brother, or sweetheart, received it come storm, snow, floods or heatwave. And if it was bad news, then Hilda had experienced that, and was in an ideal position to offer comfort and sympathy. In those days, before the telephone was the usual means of communication, letters meant such a lot. Better than a fleeting conversation, a letter could be kept and read, over and over again.

Hilda loved to deliver the post, riding her bicycle, transforming those country people's faces into wreaths of smiles as she handed over a letter or parcel, especially if it was from a beloved husband, son or brother fighting for King and Country. Payment for her services was far from queenly, 12s 6d a week, but satisfaction in the job was payment enough. After all, there wasn't much to spend money on in those quiet country districts. Especially during wartime. Indeed, everything that Hilda enjoyed was free, cycling, walking, gathering wild flowers and singing in church.

Doors stood wide open in good weather and handkerchiefs were waved in anticipation as the post girl appeared along the lanes. What fun to deliver mail to Madame Rita, the clairvoyant, 'Clocky' Taylor the watch repairer, Miss Purvis the dressmaker at her shop, Mr Bacon, the grocer, and Mr Maltby on Fishergate, every place so different.

As she continued towards Minskip, a herd of lowing cows sometimes loomed into view. Much as she loved all animals, Hilda preferred cows when there was a fence or wall between them. So she made a tactful detour down a lane that led to nowhere to avoid the confrontation. Then the farmer bellowed in amazement, 'What yer freetened of, lassie? They're more freetened o' thee.' She didn't know whether it was a compliment or not, but decided that 'discretion was the better part of valour', another of her Mama's old proverbs.

When there were letters for a farm, Hilda loitered to watch the 'pig jacks' enjoying their meal, delighting to hear their contented grunts. Far more enjoyable and natural, she thought, to nudge the others out of the way when eating and not mind what sounds emerged. Why couldn't humans be more like pigs, and not stand on ceremony so much when eating, she mused? 'Hello, horses,' she called out to those grazing in the fields. Standing her bike against a wall, she pulled a few blades of grass for them in the absence of any carrots from their garden.

Being a post girl was another kind of heaven. Being out in the fresh air, sniffing the country smells and spotting the wild flowers in springtime; the exhilarating flurry of the first snowflakes in the air, crisp leaves swirling round in autumn.

Her 'elevenses' were assured. No need to take oatcakes from home for this job. On every delivery a farmer's wife, rosy-cheeked, merry-eyed, clad in a pinafore, invited Hilda into her cosy kitchen. In the wintertime a log fire crackled cheerily, farm cats congregating round it after purring round the post girl's legs in welcome. Hilda and the farmer's wife loved to giggle. 'A telegram for you pussy, from Mr Mouse' or, 'an invitation to dine with the swine' for one of the big-eyed, curious cats.

The farmer's wife cared nothing about fashion and was, thought Hilda, somehow all the better for that. One of her husband's shirts, a comfy, hand-knitted cardigan worn over an old serge skirt, with thick lisle stockings and an ancient pair of boots sufficed. Along with a battered brown felt hat that had seen many winters.

She always had a huge piece of freshly baked apple pie, or a hunk of fruit cake on a willow-pattern plate ready for her 'young visitor' and a mug full of steaming hot cocoa. It was the highlight of Hilda's day. Her spirits sank at first if there was no post for the farm, but she needn't have worried, the farmer's wife was always on the look out for her.

'Now don't you worry if there's no post for me, Hilda love,' she told her. 'I enjoy our little chat together, so your cocoa and snack will always be waiting for you.' For, after all, even if there were no letters, the lady looked upon Hilda's visit as a mine of information about what was going on in the village, if her Dad had been troubled with any 'miscreants' and what else was going on. It certainly made a pleasant change from talking to the animals!

One day the beck had flooded down by St Helena, and Hilda had to go another way. Even so, she had to ask some workmen if they would kindly deliver the last few letters for her on the other side of the flood. They all wore big wellingtons, and were only too pleased to be of assistance. Everybody helped each other in those small country communities, no problem such that it couldn't be solved, or at least lessened, by someone.

Hilda found much amusement in her varied work too. 'Do you know what was in that parcel you brought me yesterday, Hilda?' asked one elderly lady, all agog with excitement.

What a question! The post girl didn't keep stopping to peep inside the mailbag or open corners of parcels. 'No,' replied Hilda, anticipating momentous tidings. She was ushered into the dark little cottage, taking care to haul the postbag in with her, in case some marauding animal took a fancy to it or gave itself relief on it, turning its back to it, tail a-quiver.

A brown paper parcel was laid on the table, contents spilled out for Hilda to admire. Half-a-dozen sachets of lavender and a few monogrammed handkerchiefs for her birthday, from the lady's sister in Norfolk. They smelled enchanting, and how rewarding the job was when the old lady made her accept one of the lavender sachets, 'a little thank you for being such a sweet post girl'.

After chatting for a few more minutes Hilda thanked her again, mounted her bicycle, and wended her way along the lane. She couldn't have felt happier or more content had she been the Postmaster General himself!

And oh, the health tips some of those old people passed on to her. If anyone was having a fit, tobacco smoke blown into the mouth and nostrils was supposed to bring the sufferer round. Even memory could be aided by drinking sage tea, sweetened to taste. Perspiring feet? Sprinkle oatmeal in the footwear, wrap the feet in linen, and sprinkle bran in the socks. Pillows filled with a mixture of beech leaves and the husks of oats, were the most wholesome for health, while the best remedy for 'fearful nightmares' was said to be thyme, used as a tea to promote sweet dreams.

Hilda learned from one person she delivered letters to that bunions must be painted night and morning with a tincture of iodine. For that curse of mankind, backache, a lump of common black pitch, spread on a piece of calico three-folds thick, should be applied to the back as warm as was bearable. When it fell off, the back had to be rubbed with camphorated oil.

At least, Hilda conjectured, when you were a spirit, as Ernie then was, there'd be no backache or other ills of the flesh. Besides being a wartime post girl, she was also becoming a person with a great fund of medical knowledge and home-made cures: and not one drug among them.

# OUR WOMANHOOD.

**W**OMANHOOD of homely Britain,
   High and humble, o'er the land,
We would hail your grit and courage,
   As you by the Empire stand,
While our manhood are a-fighting
And have had to leave our shore,
You've resolved to fill their places,
While the cannons loudly roar.

   *Chorus*—Thrown aside are cuffs and collars,
      Gloves and trinkets, furs and shawls,
      And for love of King and Country,
      Now you're clad in overalls.

See "Her Highness" do the nursing,
   That brings "Tommy" quickly round.
And "My Lady" acting typist,
   Farmer's daughter, till the ground,
Parlourmaid, act car-conductor,
   Cook, now drives the dairy-cart,
Sarah Jane is acting "Postie."
   While the mistress does their part.
      Chorus—

Busk the waist, who work munitions,
   Bind the locks, and tuck the sleeve,
How your hero will you worship,
   When he gets that few days' leave,
Dry the brow, and strain the muscle,
   Then no foe need us assail,
Hail again; we're debtors to ye—
   Munitioneer, or Nightingale.
      Chorus—

*Women were in great demand during the war, carrying out the jobs usually reserved for men. In her role as a wartime post girl, Hilda was certainly doing her bit for King and Country.*

# CHAPTER 26

# Rough Rider for Lord Furness

Medical knowledge was certainly needed during the awful influenza outbreak of 1918. It was worse than those scarlet fever episodes and some families, if they hadn't lost members through battle, sorrowed over those who died from the influenza. Strangely, illness came often in beautiful summertime, when one would think that only blooming roses and health were likely.

Hilda realized that the best way to get over a death in the family was not to stay at home and brood about it, but to talk to others. Her new job delivering letters and parcels was ideal therapy after the death of Ernie. What a lot of information she picked up about other people's way of life, and their way of dealing with misfortunes.

Joe Boddy, for instance, was not well-to-do but what a fascinating life he had! At one time he lived at Cundall Manor, home of Lord Furness, then joint Master of the York and Ansty hounds. He earned 25s a week, out of which he provided his own food. This was cooked in the saddle room and mainly consisted of soup, which he and the other riders cooked in a bucket. They threw in anything they could catch or 'lift' from the fields, rabbits, turnips, carrots and potatoes – a variety of ingredients. Joe reckoned those soups only cost him half-a-crown a week. Leaving him plenty over from his wage to spend on beer. Hilda's mother called such concoctions 'hash'. They were good for you and 'stuck to your ribs', especially in wintertime.

Life was hard, adventurous, but easy-going. When there were no horses to break in, and he felt like having 'a day on't spree', he simply took it. Off he went to Helperby and into the Rose and Crown, then an invigorating walk back to Cundall Manor. After a few beers, Joe delighted in riding over the jumps. He was often thrown, but he reckoned that a man didn't know what riding was if he'd not taken a fall or two. The rough riders slept in the Bothy at the Manor, keeping warm beneath twelve-foot-long horse blankets.

Joe's riding coats and corduroy breeches were tailor-made for him by Mr Steel, of Horse Fair, Boroughbridge. Joe wore fawn box-cloth leggings and black Balmoral-fronted boots with them. Lord Furness declared that he'd never seen breeches with such a perfect fit as Joe's. So Mr Steel was commissioned to make a

*The cottage in Aldborough, near Boroughbridge, where Joe Boddy lived.*

few pairs for His Lordship. An excellent pair of breeches made by him cost a guinea. Then, it wasn't quantity but quality that was the watchword. Coal was excellent. So much so that Joe boasted the riders could wash their heavy corduroys in an evening, hang them round the fire and they would be perfectly dry and ready to wear next day. Without, needless to say, any washing-machines or artificial drying aids.

'Of course,' Joe laughed as he told his tales, 'we weren't *paying* for all the coal we shovelled on.'

Even so, coal was cheap enough. On his marriage Joe went to live at Aldborough, and the young couple had a ton of bright, clean coal delivered for only a guinea. The new Mrs Boddy gave the saddler a shilling for himself, for shovelling it into the coal place. 'Grand clean logs from Ripon', make the coal last longer.

After their wedding in 1913 there was no honeymoon, Joe went fox hunting as soon as the ceremony was over. Neither he or his new wife felt the need to go away from their beloved countryside. 'We had all we wanted; plenty of furniture, plenty of good food, some hens, even a drop of whisky,' the couple often said.

During the early years of his marriage Joe rode for Mr Haswell, regularly going fox hunting. To make the coats of the horses 'shine like silver' he made linseed mash in a big iron pan, this was before the later method of feeding horses ready-made linseed cake. Much less bother, but not as good. Joe learned a great deal about the welfare of horses. For instance, a sweating horse must never be given a cold drink of water.

His most vivid memories were of the wild Canadian horses which were sent to England during the Great War. Two men had to be at Boroughbridge station to deal with each horse as it alighted. Joe then took some to Aldborough, where there were some loose boxes behind his cottage. Some he managed to tame within twenty-four hours. After making it lie on the ground, 'to let it see who was boss', he sometimes sat on the horse's head and sang to it. Any he failed to master had to be shot. (Joe Boddy's riding ability was perpetuated in his youngest son, Jack, who rode in the Grand National four times, reaching fourth place once.)

While he was out working, Mrs Boddy was busy in the cottage. Friday was baking day, when the Yorkshire range was in use from 'first thing in the morning 'till last thing at night'. What delicious aromas filled the unpolluted country air, from brown and white teacakes, huge loaves of bread, scones, buns and cakes. Often a piece of brisket, at sixpence a pound, was cooking.

Hilda was so glad that she wasn't cooped up in a factory or mill, it was delightful to be out on her bicycle, young, doing a necessary job, being told snippets of information, and best of all, breathing in those wholesome country scents.

During hot summer days Mrs Boddy took her three children to picnic by the river Ure, where they learned to swim. Always she had a stout clothes line with her, in case of difficulties. Meanwhile, Joe thoroughly enjoyed his life as a rough rider. The one time he didn't relish was Barnaby Fair, held in June. This was when the gipsies camped all the way from Boroughbridge up to Aldborough, turning their dogs and horses loose as early as three in the light mornings. The gipsies raided fields for vegetables, and milked the farmers' cows while their owners lay sleeping, unaware. Some women habitually became as drunk as the men. The many Public Houses remaining open from six in a morning till eleven at night.

But Joe, for all the roughness of his work, and low income, never dreamt of going on strike for more money. They were amply satisfied with their simple life as it was. Hilda was, too.

## CHAPTER 27

# Clem Mustill Remembered

On her daily walk to Miss West's Hilda used to pass the apartments kept by Mrs Mustill in St James's Square, advertised as having four bedrooms, two sitting-rooms, and being 'pleasantly situated'. A Miss Rowley also had apartments up New Row where Hilda lived, with two bedrooms, two sitting-rooms, a piano, and dinners and teas provided. Tourists were fascinated to go to the area because of the Devil's Arrows and the beautiful, peaceful surroundings.

*Clem Mustill, a youthful portrait.*

*Clem Mustill at Boroughbridge in 1989.*

**Mustill's**

**MINERAL WATER WORKS**

Boroughbridge.

*Syphons, Stone Ginger Beer,*
*Cordials, &c.*

AGENT FOR

*High-Class Vinegars.*

*Clem's family business was an integral part of Boroughbridge life when Hilda lived there.*

Mustill's also had a mineral water works, and were firewood merchants. Their grandson, Clem, lived with his parents at a house named Hazel Dene in Aldborough until 1913, when they moved to Boroughbridge.

During school holidays, Clem helped at the mineral water works for pocket money. It was then that he first saw Hilda, the milliner's apprentice, on that morning when she walked down New Row to begin working for Miss West.

'She gave me such a lovely smile,' Clem told me years afterwards. A smile that spanned the years, for although he never spoke to her, he never forgot her or the Haigh family. Therefore how delighted he was to see an article I had published in *The Dalesman* a few years ago, and a photograph of the family who had once lived so near to his.

He wrote to me, and we arranged to meet. Clem, then a lively old gentleman carrying a bright red walking stick, asked me to stand at the exact spot down New Row where, during the Great War, he first saw and admired the young milliner's apprentice. I wore a long, Laura Ashley-type skirt to try and resemble the one Mother wore all those years ago. After he had taken the photograph, Clem proved to be as wonderful a storyteller as she had been.

He remembered the bottling machine at the mineral water works, consisting of a column round which bottles were moved on a rotating plate. The plate was recessed to allow for the insertion and removal of bottles by hand. Bottles moved under a nozzle for filling. The operator wore gloves, also a mask to protect himself against burst bottles. The steam engine was a single cylinder, medium-speed steam being supplied from a vertical boiler. A hot-water tank with rotating nozzles and revolving brushes was used for cleaning the bottles. Dandelion and Burdock, lemonade and ginger beer were firm favourites. Mustill's were also agents for Cambrian vinegar.

Deliveries were made to outlying towns and villages such as Topcliffe and Easingwold by horse-drawn wagon at first. Then the firm progressed to a second-hand motor van, wooden crates rattling along in the back. Mustill's apartments and mineral water works were advertised in the book, *The Abbey Vale of Lower Yore*.

Clem's grandma, Martha Shirley Mustill, died in 1912, and her grave is in Boroughbridge cemetery across the road from the church. It is not far from the graves of Sarah Eleanor, Arthur William, and their son Ernest R. Haigh. The latter decorated with the insignia of the West Yorkshire Regiment.

Schooldays for Clem began in Miss Thompson's 'Dame' school, prior to the rough and tumble of Boroughbridge School. At the latter, Mr Mawer was the Headmaster, and boys thought up imaginative ways of dodging the severity of being caned. Some put horse hair across the palm of their hands, while one lad slipped a tin tray down his trousers before a whacking. 'It sounded like a kettledrum,' laughed Clem. Another boy screamed in terror when due for a caning, 'I'm dead!' 'This'll bring you to life again,' sardonically replied the teacher, twirling the cane. Another time a lad was ordered to lean over the desk. He leaned the wrong way. Clem burst out laughing and was caned as well for seeing the joke.

Boys were occasionally sent down to the river to cut willow for canes, they wore them out so fast. Girls who misbehaved were never punished physically, well, they weren't supposed to be. They were made to stay behind after school was over. No wonder Grandma Mustill offered sixpence to the first child to learn the Lord's Prayer, to try and instill a bit of seemly behaviour in them.

In 1915, Clem, with other boy scouts, went camping in the Lake District with Scout Master Sydney Padgett. Then there was Scout Master Dixon, who used to read Conan Doyle's, *The Speckled Band* as they sat round the camp fire. He also made up a ditty, 'You can take a weekend trip to the village of Minskip, Oh, what a happy folk we are'. Clem didn't remember the rest of it, but he fancied himself a poet too.

When Clem was a pupil at Harrogate Grammar School, the boys were invited to try writing a 'tender poem'. A bit of a romantic, Clem dreamed up 'Sweet Sophia':

> Of all the girls that I take out
> There's none like Sweet Sophia,
> I wander round the town and sigh, and wonder what to buy her,
> Her neck is like a Periscope, her face as red as fire.
> Ah, oft I wonder what to do, to win my Sweet Sophia.
> One summer's even, as true love's token,
> I took her to a picture show, which left me stoney broken,
> I went into a chocolate shop, and when I did retire
> Alas, I found a rival bold, had walked off with Sophia.

Thus versified the budding poet.

In 1919 Police Constable Haigh retired, and took the family to live in Huddersfield, where he took up the position of a security officer at L.B. Holliday. Never dreaming of owning a car, this move was akin to removing to the other side of the world. Goodbye meant goodbye to most people then if they lived more than a few miles away. Clem Mustill never saw Hilda or any of the Haighs again.

*The last photograph to be taken of Grandma Haigh, here with Hilda in 1942. They are in the field at the back of Central Stores, Deighton. This is where Hilda then lived and Grandma was visiting.*

But the same kind of life continued. That year the Ouseburne Choral Society went to sing in Boroughbridge, the conductor Miss Hardcastle held her baton high and the floor collapsed; the soprano, a hefty lady, was suddenly concealed up to her chest, mouth still wide open.

Then there was the forgetful Reverend Gamallial Milner, Vicar of Roecliffe in the 1920s, who frequently forgot his sermon. Once he asked the station master, 'where do I want to go?' More than once he cycled to Boroughbridge, then, in a daydream, walked back afterwards, leaving the bicycle propped up somewhere there. But in those days such happenings weren't given frightening medical names, but simply regarded as a bit of harmless eccentricity.

Music played a great part in Clem's life, as it did in my mother's. Clem recalled 'The Nightbirds Jazz Band' with drummer Jazzy Knowlson, known as the boy who brought jazz to the Dales, and Jack Broadwith at the piano. Then there were Albert Swift, Artie Buck and their bands. One Sunday, Thirsk Band was booked to give a Sacred Concert. To everyone's amazement, towards the close, Jazzy Knowlson couldn't resist leading the players with 'Home, in Pasadena'. The audience, though some wouldn't admit it, loved it.

Ada Wrack, daughter of the Police Sergeant who followed Sergeant Foster, became a professional singer. Police Constable Haigh's daughters, Hilda and Ella, both had exceptionally glorious contralto voices. Ella had singing lessons, eventually winning the Mrs Sunderland Rose Bowl in the Huddersfield competition. It must have been the pure, unsullied air of their childhood that filled their lungs. Even the tramps sang and whistled. Clem remembered one in particular who roamed the countryside, forever singing, 'When the Fields are White With Daisies'.

Open-air dances were enjoyed in a field behind the gate known as Nanny Pit, a regular meeting place for young people. One just had to take pot luck if a lavatory was needed, as there weren't any. On Saturday evenings there were 'bob hops' at Aldborough. A stove provided warmth, but as the evening wore on and passions flared, the graveyard inevitably became fuller! 'Some of the goings-on would have had to be written on asbestos,' Clem laughed.

But it was a marvellous era. Young men wore their best suits and a pianist played hits of the day: 'Keep the Home Fires Burning', 'Roses of Picardy', 'A Brown Bird Singing' and 'Mademoiselle from Armentiers, Inky, Pinky, Parlez-vous'. Those high-spirited youths and young ladies danced to the Tinkle Tankle Foxtrot, the Eva Three Step, and, in the Lancers, the great boast was to swing the girls horizontal, or at least until they were completely dizzy. Sometimes they had a go at the 'Cake Walk'.

'May I have the pleasure?' was the well-brought-up young gentleman's way of inviting the lady of his choice to dance. If he wished to remain with one particular girl he bribed the pianist to keep on playing longer than usual. Could Heaven have anything fairer than to be with the girl of your dreams for the last waltz?

Clem had special affection for the Christmas parties that were held towards the close of the First World War, also the Fancy Dress Balls. There was fortune telling, musical chairs, and, best of all, postman's knock. Although Clem admitted that sometimes kissing a girl was more like kissing a brick. But the young district nurse was always asked to dance, 'because you never knew when you might need her'.

There were plenty of girls to choose from, as so many young men never returned from the war. The Ramsdale girls, whose father had a butcher's shop in the Square. Mr Bacon, the grocer, had three charming daughters, including Mary and Edna. Doctor Daggett's daughter, Ethel, later married the then Bishop of Coventry. Then there was Eve Easterby, who had a motor bike, and once gave Clem a ride on the pillion. He was a guest at her twenty-first birthday party and proposed her health on her eightieth.

Tennis parties in the 1920s were held at Ladywell House. There were cricket and hockey teams to join, concerts and plays to act in. Once, Miss Thwaites, a very refined lady, was cast to play Abraham Lincoln in the absence of any suitable gentleman actor. Unfortunately, nothing would induce her to wear trousers on stage. How the ungodly roared with laughter when 'Abraham Lincoln' appeared on the stage in a skirt!

Entertainment of quite another kind was the occasional menageries held in the Gipsy Field, rented out by Joseph Mustill. There were moth-eaten lions and other 'wild beasts'. Not least among the latter were local lads with ropes and nooses who, cowboy fashion, lassoed the girls or anybody unfortunate enough to be in the vicinity. Occasionally, to add to the din, a cannon roared.

Clem told me about the Portable Cinema in 1918, and solo pianist Mary Tilburn. In later years there were Montgomery's silent films in the Public Hall to be marvelled at. They advertised one of the most up-to-date sets in Yorkshire. When the pianist began there was an accompaniment from the audience, howls, screams, cat calls and whistles of sheer excitement and exuberance at the novelty of it all.

*The wedding of Hilda Haigh and Joe Taylor in 1923. Grandma Haigh is sitting third left on the first row with her husband, Grandad Haigh, standing behind her. Grandma Taylor is sitting second right on the first row with her husband, Grandad Taylor, wearing the splendid top hat, standing behind her. Winnie is sitting next to Grandma Taylor and Ella is sitting to the right of the bride. Law Taylor, who was to be Mayor of Huddersfield from 1924 to 1926, is standing on the far right of the back row.*

Clem became Managing Director of the Leeds firm, Jackson Boilers. In 1929 he married Marion Harrison, of Pately Bridge, who was a gifted pianist. Their son, Michael, is now Lord Justice Mustill. Hilda, transplanted to Huddersfield, married Dad, Joe Taylor, in 1923. He had taken over his parents grocery business when his brother Alfred was killed during the war. Well, he died of 'spotted fever' which amounts to the same thing; the war ultimately caused his death. Hilda could pop into town on a tramcar and buy hats galore if she fancied them. Even so, she always liked adding a few touches of her own, a flower here, or a bit of veiling and velvet. She gave her 'old' hats to customers who couldn't afford to buy their own, thus having an excellent excuse to buy a new hat for herself.

It was a busy life at the shop, and to me, Boroughbridge and her life there seemed to be more of a Shangri La, a Lost Horizon; not a real place. Especially as we never had a car and bus journeys took so long.

So, coming up for Christmas in 1971, I wrote to the *Yorkshire Post*, enclosing a photograph of Hilda when she was Miss West's apprentice. I wrote that we hoped to take Mother, who by that time had been twice widowed, to visit the beloved haunts of her childhood. Did anybody still remember her? Shoals of letters arrived, *of course* they remembered Hilda and would love to see her again.

*Hilda in Boroughbridge on Christmas morning in 1971.*

We went by bus that Christmas Eve day and stayed at the Crown Hotel. That evening our first call was to visit Emily Robinson. Mother, slightly agitated, wondered how to introduce herself after all those years.

We knocked at the door. It opened, and a smiling Emily stood there. 'Oh, good evening,' Mother said, 'I'm the late Hilda Haigh.' Well, poor Emily must have thought she was playing a part in Dickens' *A Christmas Carol* and Marley's ghost had turned up on the doorstep. The ice was broken at once, everyone erupting into gales of laughter as we were ushered inside. Over the next day or two we visited the police station, the cemetery where Ernie, Sarah Eleanor and Arthur William were buried, and even went inside Jasmine Cottage. We had invitations to tea and reminiscences. So bemused was Hilda at actually walking up New Row again that when she took her coat off, her scarlet Christmas Day jumper had been pulled on inside out, with the label showing.

It was the best Christmas for years, even though there were no pink or white sugar pigs to fight over. Hilda had so many memories of those halcyon, golden days, when girls wore pretty dresses and enormous picture hats, when there were romantic, lilting songs to dance to, so many happy memories. Among the happiest for Clem, however, was the never-to-be-forgotten moment when the village constable's daughter, Hilda, smiled at him as she walked down New Row to begin her first day as a milliner's apprentice.